Thank You (s)

2nd edition –To my sweet husband Oscar, a special thank you for your patience with me. I require a lot of patience. You covered me with your love.

1st edition - Thank you Marcie Eanes for your talent as copy editor.

Thank you Georgia D. Washington for your consistent encouragement.

Thank you Joseph Beckles for your overwhelming inspiration.

Thank you Val Ayres-Dawson for your continuous insight.

A very special thanks to my sons, Rogelio and Roshard. Thank you for your love and support.

Thank you to me myself and I for our continuous commitment to learning, working through the challenges and moving on.

Love is the key...

Gratitude

There are some people that I want to thank for making this book possible. I want to first thank my friend Derrick who kept my yard cut and trees trimmed at no charge.

Next I want to thank Mary Ann for the free house cleaning service. It was nice to come home from work each day and never have to worry about cleaning the house. Special thanks go to Wilma for completely taking over the responsibility of cooking for myself and my son, Roshard.

My car needed an oil change and Marcus took over that for me. I don't know how I would have been able to finish this book, if I had to do all the things I normally do. Marcus went even further. He washed my car every week without being asked. Now that's something to get excited about!!

I am a member of a few organizations and hold a number of positions. My friends in these organizations took over my duties for six months so I could write. With so many people ensuring my success, I could not fail! Mary Ann, Derrick and Marcus DO NOT EXIST. I made up these friends for the purpose of making a point.

If you wait for a picture perfect set of circumstances, you will never live your dreams. You must decide

Gratitude

how you will use your time. *You have but one life to live, so what will it be?*

Where To Find It

Where To Find It

Not Everyone Will Like You

You Don't Have To Stay
Between The Lines

Don't Let Your Limitations Limit You

You Can Live A Rich Life Without Being Rich

Where To Find It

Introduction

This introduction is dedicated to Valerie Ayres-Dawson. If it were not for her, this introduction would never have been written.

Does your life need a plunger? Is your life stopped up? Are you just going through the motions of life? Is your life barely moving through its clogged drain? Do you want your life to flow?

Stop, here it is. My sincere desire is for you to enjoy this book and keep it as a plunger when your life gets stopped up. Where can you find the formula for living your life? There is no magic here; just a simple girl from Los Angeles living her life. In this book I will share my story.

My experience is simply that, my experience. When you finish reading this book, you will know if you are living your life. Of course, you must want to know! The stories are great, however living your life is personal. It's your choice......

I loved to write and I wanted to be around others who shared my passion for poetry. In 1995 I wrote a number of poems and I was excited. A few months later, I mentioned to a friend that I wanted to join a local poetry group. Much to my surprise and delight she replied, "I know one." She gave me the telephone number and the rest is history.

Introduction

I joined The Writer's Corner poets in 1996 and remained a member until I moved out of the area. I wrote dozens and dozens of poems over the next few years. It seems that poetry would be my first book, but I was wrong. After I completed the book of poetry, I wasn't excited. Being excited is definitely a good sign for me. I still have that book. Maybe one day I'll get back to it.

Creating my own templates for my custom greeting cards and bookmarks required many hours of tedious work, but I enjoyed every minute.

Somehow in the midst of all of this, my life found time to be depressed. I can't explain it, but it happened. Depression had come to visit. It took a very long time for me to realize that I was depressed. During this episode, I constantly battled the demons of depression. By continuing to keep moving, I was able to keep depression from stopping me.

Having read how serious depression can be; I fought back with every weapon at my disposal. I went to plays, music concerts, museums and did everything that I enjoy to fight my way out of depression. I was so depressed that I scared myself. I'd experienced slight depression from time to time, but never had it lasted so long. I didn't lock myself away from friends and family nor did I give up any of my

Introduction

activities. I was in a dark place inside myself with no answers as to how I got there and how to get out. I felt lost and afraid. I was angry at myself because I could not figure out how I came to this place.

My life was full of things that I enjoyed. So why did depression knock on my door? I can't explain it. The longer the depression lasted the more frightened I became. What else could I do? I called the employee assistance program and made an appointment to see a counselor. It always helps to talk to a trained professional. This total period of extreme depression lasted well over a year (1996-1997). There was no one event that caused the depression but several. As usual, I took on too much responsibility for my family and friends.

I was determined to continue to focus on my own talents. I knew that determination had served me well in the past and continues to be my corner stone. While creating and having fun, I still wanted to do something else.

I've loved to write all of my life and little did I know where that would lead. Writing for me was a way to express myself in a very personal and frank way. I wrote for myself and didn't share much with anyone. However, I had forgotten the times I wrote 20 page letters. I wrote over 100 letters in length of 8-20 pages.

I started to recall feedback from different people. Over the years, many individuals said to me, "You should write that down, write that down." The record started to play over and over again, "Write about what you know."

Suddenly in 1999 things started to fall into place. I knew that the best way to get started writing a book was to just put all my thoughts into my lap top without trying to analyze every word. My next challenge was finding time to write a book. I didn't get very far in 1999 because of my busy schedule.

In 2000, another brainstorm blew into town (my head). The MLK, Jr. three-day weekend was coming up and I'd devote it to writing. I came up with a plan. I told family and friends that I was going out of town for the weekend. I was determined to devote the time to writing.

I renamed my family room, Shirley's Hotel. My youngest son (18 years old) was still living at home and I told him that I was not available to him unless it was an emergency. He said, cool! I set up camp in my family room. My laptop and I had a date. The weekend turned out to be a stroke of genius. I wrote and wrote and wrote. The major part of this book was written in that three-day weekend.

I had no idea how many rewrites were ahead of me before I had a finished product. How many? There were too many to count. I hired Marcie Eanes a talented editor and inspirational poet.

When I arrived home from work, my real job started. I live my dreams every day. Whether I am awake or asleep, my dreams are the same. Some days I'd write all evening into the early morning hours. Many mornings I'd fell asleep around 1:00 or 2:00 a.m. Then get up at 5:30 a.m., to be at work by 7:00 a.m. Then on other occasions, I'd go to sleep at 10:00 p.m. and wake up between 2:30 a.m. and 3:30 a.m. This book would not leave me alone so I had to complete it.....

Some people start living their lives earlier than others. It is never too late.

I am amazed when people comment on the many attributes they see in me. The attributes are correct but should include my challenges as well, such as, negative thinking, self-doubt, pity parties and depression.

Introduction

A rich life is around the corner. If you wear expensive clothes, drive an expensive car, live in an expensive house and make a lot of money, it doesn't mean you are living your life. Life may be dragging you along. If you earn minimum wage, ride the bus and live in an apartment, it doesn't mean you aren't living your life. You are the only one who knows if you are living your life.

Ask yourself a few questions. Who are you? What do you want to do with your life? Do you have peace in your spirit? Who are you really? Life can't drag you along if you are living a rich life. If you don't know who you really are, then life is dragging you along. You could live to be 100 and still not live your life.

Your occupation, financial status nor your bloodline can prevent you from living a rich life. The choice is yours. A rich life is around the corner. When you turn the corner, you will find the you that you never knew.

Challenges don't stop when you live a rich life, it is an opportunity to make a conscious decision to continue living a rich life. There is a season for everything. All of my experiences contribute to living my rich life.

My sweet husband Oscar Lee Cormia
A gift from God to me

The day we met is crystal clear. I drove into the parking lot for Jazz at Drew. The parking lot was empty except for one other car. I parked where I could see the gate and get in line quickly. As I sat in my car waiting for the gate to open, another vehicle pulled into the parking lot. The truck backed into the space right next to me.

When I existed my car, I had to walk pass the truck and made eye to eye contact with the driver. Oh, what beautiful eyes. His eyes sucked me in. I tried not to blush but I could not control myself. He said hello and I replied hello and moved quickly across the street to enter the concert grounds.

He found me inside the concert and introduced himself, Oscar Cormia. We both were meeting friends at the concert. Once the concert started, we ignored our friends and spent most of the day together talking and getting to know each other.

We were inseparable from that day forward. We discovered we were both praying for a special someone and God answered our prayers. Four years later, we were married.

Live Your Life

Or

Life Will Drag

You Along...

Learning

As

You

Go

Fair

I am sure you've heard this statement, "What makes you think life is supposed to be fair!" Now let's think about fair. What is fair? How can you measure fair? How will you recognize fair? Do you really want fair?

Fair is what you think fair is. If you think it's fair for you to get paid for 40 hours when you only worked 30, then that's fair. If 100 people were asked to define fair, there would be 100 different answers.

I define fair as accepting responsibility for making choices. Making choices is very important to living a fair life. Thus, choices set the pace and tone for life. Most important, be fair to yourself........Being fair to yourself means loving yourself even when you don't like some of the choices you've made. Fair mean you keep going because you realize there are always new choices to be made. Choose to block out the negative comments that people throw your way.

Don't receive everything that comes your way. Some people are good at draining your energy. Stay away from energy draining people! Create your own world within the larger world. Spend time with people who encourage you. Fair means being able to encourage yourself. Fair means the world is your oyster. Reach for the other limits of your imagination. Fair means more. More peace of mind, more contentment and more of everything that is good for you. When you do this, you will be free of your ankle weights. Now you can be all that you can be and achieve your dreams.

When you choose to live a fair life, you will be challenged. Don't turn back. People operate on many different systems. You will meet those who do not understand your choices and that is fair. It is not their life, it is your life. The most important issue is your emotional well being. Therefore, take a deep breath, hold it for a few seconds and blow it out. *Ah, to live a fair life or not, that is the question. That is fair.*

Invitation

You're feeling great so you decide to have a few friends over for fun and food. You plan the menu and send out the invites. It's always great to get friends together for no special occasion.

On the day of the party, everyone is talking, sharing, eating and laughing. Most of them know each other. They haven't seen each other for a long time. Friends catch up on family weddings, kids' softball games, orthodontist adventures and which kids have crossed into the dreaded "dating" phase.

The discussion then turns to the changes that occur as one gets older. Of course, the first topic was hair. Everyone gets into the act. Which person has the most gray hair and who doesn't have any hair at all.

Included in the invitation was a request to bring family pictures. Everyone remembered to bring pictures and they brought the most laughter and sharing of the evening. Lots of ah, ooh, how cute and he looks just like his Dad. By this time you are really pleased with yourself. You think to yourself, boy this was a great idea, I'm glad I did it.

The invitation stated the time of the party as 2:00-6:00 p.m. Some people left by 6:00 p.m. but a few lingered on and on. They just did not want to go home. At first thought, it may seem that some of

Invitation

your friends are inconsiderate of your time. It's always good to reconsider your conclusions. This gives you an opportunity to see if the result is the same.

Is it possible that some people desperately needed the friends' get-together? They do not want to leave, not your house, but the environment of companionship, conversation and sense of belonging.

Your invitation accomplished more than you ever thought it would. This "no special occasion" gathering has given many something they needed. They think if they stay longer, they can hold onto the good feelings. Good feelings are important to everyone and we never seem to get enough of them.

When was the last time you had friends over just for fun, no special occasion? It doesn't even have to be at your home. Go to a coffee house or restaurant. Reconnect with family and friends.

Everyone had a great time and they are looking forward to the next get together.

Write an invite today.

Mail

When I walk in the house, I pick up the mail and immediately start sorting it. I need to keep the mail congestion from building up and this is not easy. So much information comes at me every day that I need to control the intake as much as possible.

Anyone who feels lonely or unimportant because the only mail they receive are bills should celebrate. Once your name gets on one mailing list, that equals another and another. It just keeps multiplying. Pretty soon you either think that you are pretty important or someone wants to make your life miserable. Playing at your house, "Attack of the Mail."

I tried separating the mail into these categories, yes, no and maybe. Well I still got a headache because that means that I had to go through the mail a second and third time before deciding what to do. Yuk!

Then, another idea came to mind. Trash all mail right away unless it was bills. Doing this sounds good in theory, but was not a practical solution for me. For example, I receive newsletters, periodicals and such that I wanted to read at a later date. So, I decided on several more categories: reading materials, social events, file and require response. Boy this proved to be a headache too.

Mail

When I was really busy, I sorted the mail two ways; trash immediately and maybe. This worked really well for a long time. I still had to come back and look at the maybe mail and that was a huge stack.

Finally I decided on my present method of **mail elimination**. I picked up the mail when I walk into the house, separated bills into one stack and started to scan the rest. If it's bulk mail or there's no return address, it's trashed. Next, if I did open it, I'd read a few lines and decide whether to throw it away or not. Those times when I was extremely over-taxed, I trashed even my favorite newsletters, periodicals and such. It's not the end of the world if I don't read these things. What I don't know, I can't miss.....

If it's an event that I plan to attend, I secure it on the refrigerator with a magnet. If the invitation requires an RSVP, I called immediately.

Mail

Sometimes you don't realize how little things like mail can clutter your house and most importantly, your mind. Sit down, think about it and ask yourself this question. Which will it be, *mail elimination or mail constipation?*

Partners

I've formed two business partnerships that taught me a few things. The most important lesson learned was that things are not always what they seem on the surface.

One such partnership was a real estate investment. The four of us started out very excited about our partnership. We all professed that we wanted to see **our business** grow into financial success. I soon learned my first lesson. Our partnership was very good in the beginning. **However,** that premise looked entirely different when we actually started working. A partnership will not survive if individual goals become the primary focus. When all went well, we were one big happy family. When things fell apart, so did our big happy family.

Financial challenges came up early and proved to be a sticking point for all. We couldn't agree on the solution.

You don't really know how a person will respond to adversity until adversity rears its ugly head. Believe me, it will! I am sure you've read in the newspaper about executives who worked for multi-million dollar companies and ended up in a court of law to settle financial differences. Some of our country's most lucrative business partnerships have ended in a blaze of conflict. Guess what? They had some of the greatest legal minds design air tight contracts. So what is an air tight contract? There is no such animal!

When entering into a partnership, there are a few things that will increase your chances of success. Nothing is conflict proof. Have a lawyer write a contract for you and develop a business plan. Work together from the very first phase.

Of course, there are dozens of books that offer expert details on business partnerships. Please invest in a few of them. You'll be glad you did. Better yet, check out a few at the library and decide which ones you like before making a purchase.

I learned that it is very important to spend time working side by side with your partners. This is your best defense .

If you have taken time to get to know your partners, you've seen them in many different situations. Just asking a person how they would handle a hypothetical situation is *not sufficient*. Actions speak louder than words.

Each personality within your partnership should compliment one other. If you cannot discuss the difficult issues beforehand, you are already in deep

Partners

trouble. These suggestions will help prevent the demise of your partnership. *Choose all your partnerships very carefully.*

Practice

Practice until you get it. Remember when you repeated your ABCs until you memorized them? You wrote your name over and over and over until you could write it with your eyes closed. I believe everything is practice. It takes more than reading a thing once to get it and especially to keep it.

I practice how I want to live my life. At the top of my practice list is how I want to start each day. I want to start each day excited. I tell myself that it is a good day and start working in that direction. I have practiced this for so many years, it's second nature. It doesn't mean that everything is going my way. It does mean that I have chosen to have a great day.

I want to feel physically good so I start my day with exercise. This is a good way to wake up and get the old body working.

Practice has taught me that I can develop habits that I choose and learn new skills. Whenever I learn a new computer system, I practice and practice until it becomes second nature.

When I read "Don't Sweat The Small Stuff" by Richard Carlson I responded, "absolutely." Prior to reading his book, I already practiced this philosophy. The book is full of excellent examples. This does not mean I always accomplish it, but I do more

Practice

often than not. Therefore, I still practice.

What do you want to do? Whatever it is, you can do it. *It's your choice, start practicing today.*

Self Sufficient

I do not believe anyone is self sufficient. I don't believe anyone can live without being dependent on others for something. Of course how much dependency and how often varies drastically. People say that I am self sufficient and I suppose it does look that way. Of course it is not so. I need lots of people.

I need people to listen to my concerns, to exchange ideas, to encourage me, to go out to dinner with, to laugh with and especially to love.

Self-sufficient has many definitions and has generated many steamy conversations and debates. For this book, self-sufficient is defined as relying upon oneself to live a loving life. Living a loving life is up to me. I do the things that bring love into my life. I dance whenever I feel like it because I love to dance. I surround myself with books I love, music I love, pictures I love and people that I love. Self-sufficient means I am qualified and competent to determine what I need in my life.

Self sufficient does not mean that I don't need hugs. I absolutely need hugs all the time. I need friends to share in the enjoyment of plays, concerts, vacations, etc. I enjoy my alone time and seek to maintain my life's rhythm (balance). Am I self-sufficient? Yes. *Does that mean I don't need people? No.*

Single Parent

Men are so smart. They never try to do everything. When a man is a single parent, their approach is much less stressful than a single mom. Of course, being a single parent automatically brings a great deal of responsibility, but they do not try to be super Dads.

What does being super parent mean? That's a person who bakes cookies for school, sells candy for Little League and cleans the entire house every weekend. Let's not forget participating in the neighborhood beautification projects, sharing car pool duties to dance class, washing and ironing clothes and on and on. You get the picture.

As a single mom, I loved to cook for my sons. Of course people failed to acknowledge the fact that I too like home cooked meals. I cooked several meals on weekend and put the food in microwave dinner plates. When we came home in the evening, my sons could go to the refrigerator and get dinner. This practice served me very well for many years.

At the beginning of each week, I made my schedule of meetings/lessons/practices for church, school, sports, block club, household chores, etc., etc., etc. I gave myself a lot to do and tried to accomplish it all. Now how crazy was that?

Now the single dads I know handle things quite differently. They start each day just happy they got the kids off to school. They do not concern themselves with planning meals. When the evening comes, then they figure out what they will eat.

The last pair of socks may be worn before Dad gets around to washing clothes. On top of that, if Dad doesn't get around to washing socks, he'll buy new ones. I worked hard at trying to duplicate their approach, however I did not succeed. Men are more likely to take things as they come and not sweat the small stuff. It's this approach that does not add to an already demanding job.

I would sweat over everything. Bad! I was constantly trying new strategies to help organize my days and lessen the stress on me that often spilled over onto my sons. A better approach is to make a list of things that you think need to be done.

Sometimes looking at the items on paper make things easier to see. Next, start crossing items off. This exercise allows you to really determine what is necessary for your family. The list will be different for each family. The idea here is to realize that you cannot do what two parents would do and remain sane. No, even when you drive yourself crazy, you cannot do what two parents do.

Single Parent

For example, you may put your children's rehearsals and practices at the top of the list. Whatever is important, relax with that. Keep the entire list to remind you what is really important. Put this list on your refrigerator. You need to see what is important so that you do not try to make everything important.

Each day will present its own list. I noticed that my list became shorter and shorter over the years. If your revised list looks very short, don't worry. Unplanned items will occur each day!

That is why it's so important to keep the list short. Being a single parent is a tremendously challenging job; *cut yourself some slack*!

Dedicated to everyone...................

Why

Why sing
  To touch
Why dance
  To paint
Why laugh
  To enjoy
Why cry
  To release
Why listen
  To learn
Why talk
  To connect
Why write
  To express
Why despair
  To recognize
Why curious
  To discover
Why silent
  To relax
Why hate
  NO REASON

3-16-16
Shirley A. Smith

Stress Buster

The other day I was really upset with my youngest son and I wanted to "tell him off." However, he was asleep, so I had to wait. I wanted to remind him how important it is to take good care of my car. Of course, he does not agree that the car is mine, even though he had not completed paying for it.

While I was driving around alone running errands, I started talking to my son and telling him off. What a wonderful release. It was so funny as I was talked to myself (which I always do) getting things off my chest. This greatly reduced my stress level. Of course, I cannot repeat the things I said, but it was great fun. I like my new found method of releasing stress.

A few days later, my son and I were in the car together on a rare occasion. As we were riding and talking, the subject of taking care of his car came up. I told him how I released stress by telling him off when I was alone in my car. He just thought that was so funny. He laughed and I laughed, we laughed and laughed.

Step right up and get your safe, clean and free stress buster. This method has earned four stars with environmental organizations. Get in your Car and tell someone off, even if it happens to be you! *This is big time fun.*

Tough Job

What has been my toughest job? I always answered, raising my sons. Of course as time has rolled along, I find that no longer holds true. The toughest job is raising myself. That's right, myself. I thought it was tough trying to keep up with two schools, art lessons, Boy Scouts, choir rehearsal, basketball, track, PTA, football and more.

I thought tough was when both schools and the sports programs had fund-raisers at the same time. I tried to split co-workers, family and friends into, please-buy-this-stuff groups. I tried but failed. There were never enough people to purchase all that I had to sell.

When it was time for me to sleep, I always found myself checking my list twice. Tomorrow is practice, dinner is prepared and in the refrigerator.

Are lunches ready? Are book bags packed?   I thought those were tough years. Don't get me wrong they were challenging, but not as challenging as "I am!"

I realize that there is so much emotional confusion going on inside me, that I have a job for life. Talk about a tough job. There is only one who is *equipped to handle this tough job, and that's God.*

Traffic Jam

I write because I must. If I didn't write out my thoughts, I'd go nuts!! Of course, I am crazy, just not as crazy as I could be. When I don't transfer thoughts out, I get pretty confused. Mental traffic jams erupt because my thoughts begin fighting for space.

Did you ever begin a sentence and couldn't complete it? Happens to me all the time. Can't find the end of the sentence anywhere in my head. It gets worse. I've been known to begin a sentence and before I can complete it, I'll begin another one. This has proved to be a great source of embarrassment for me and amusement for others. Trying to explain what just happened is impossible, therefore I just laugh.

If I write down my appointments, it relieves overcrowding my mind. Keeping a planning calendar helps reduce mental fatigue. I write down things I plan to do, people I want to call, positive messages to myself and more. These are few things I take care of immediately. The sole purpose of this process is to avoid mental traffic jams.

The more things you have on your mind at one time, the more inattentive you are. You're less patient and more anxious. This is a formula for arguments, upset stomach, heartburn/headaches, anxiety and depression.

Traffic Jam

Toss out the garbage in your head. Grab a pen and paper or use a computer to write away the excess. Either way, it's a win, win situation. Close the document without saving it.

Of course, if you don't have a computer, be very careful about writing down your thoughts because someone might find the paper. You should discard it immediately.

The idea is to get it out of your head and be done with it. Wouldn't it be wonderful to get rid of 90% of unwanted, unnecessary, energy draining thoughts? This is great! The reason I say 90% instead of 100% is because there will be 10% that will not be so easy to get rid of, however 90% is wonderful. That frees up space in your head for positive, peaceful, useful thoughts.

Your thoughts can be a major source of confusion in your life. Let the traffic flow smoothly. *Traffic control your life before things ride out of control.*

Wish Them Well

When you wish someone well, you have done the best you can do. When and if you find relationships (family and/or friends) leaving you drained, you have decisions to make.

Ask yourself a few questions: Are you drained after spending time with them? Is this a frequent occurrence? Can you limit your interactions with the person? Make some choices and develop boundaries for your relationships. Choose how much time, if any, you want to spend with each person. You may find you enjoy one hour with a person versus four hours. No matter your decision, "Wish Them Well."

Making a decision means that you are not resentful or angry. Clarifying relationships will greatly improve your peace of mind, reduce anxiety and stress.

Both you and the individual gain from setting boundaries. You recognize that you are just as important as everyone else. You have taken a position and shared it with the individuals. The other person does not have to accept your boundaries; however, this is not your problem. Wish them well. Whatever they choose will not impact your decision. The reason for establishing boundaries is to wish both yourself and them well.

Wish Them Well

It may be more difficult to do this with a family member or childhood friend. Dwanye's mother took a great deal of pride in her cooking and especially her prized pecan pie. Often she mentioned how much he liked her pecan pie and she enjoyed baking for him.

One Christmas, she baked a whole pecan pie for him to take home. She absolutely knew he loved pecan pie. When Dwayne arrived home, he threw the entire pie in the garbage. Dwayne hated pecan pie, but never had the courage to tell his mother the truth. Therefore he chose to let her waste her time and money rather than take the chance she'd get angry. Dwayne never told his mother the truth about anything.

The fear of hurting someone's feelings can hold you back from making small choices as well as large ones. Do you want to move to another city? Are you looking for a career change? The barber has a chair and clippers just waiting to cut your hair. That butterfly tattoo is calling your name. *On your mark, get ready, set, go! Live your life.*

Sit

A

Spell

Think of your emotional stability as a bank account. Do you make regular deposits or just withdrawals? If you don't make deposits, you will soon have a zero balance when stuff starts to happen in your life. Deposits make it possible to ride out these episodes with relative ease. The optimum word, relative! The question is, have you built a safety net for your life?

What's a safety net? A net to catch you when life presents the inevitable. You receive a two-day turn off notice from the water company. You thought you paid the bill. Not to panic, the payment is recorded in your checkbook. But after a thorough search of your record book, you don't find a check written to the water company.

A message on your voicemail says your daughter missed the first three days of summer school. The two make up classes are mandatory to graduate. You thought she was going to summer school every day.

You finally decide to get back to the remainder of the mail. The water company bill was pink therefore it caught your attention immediately.

Your new mortgage company wants to come out and inspect the property within the next two weeks. The gardener forgot to bill you last month, therefore, the present bill is for two months.

The work day was long and challenging. Ten minutes earlier you thought how nice it was to be home. That was before you listened to your voicemail and opened your mail. This is when you need to make an emotional withdrawal.

Occasionally, it's a good idea to check your emotional bank account. You don't want to get caught short because this is one account you'll always need.

Every time you take time out to go the movie, walk along the beach, ready a book, watch sports, go camping or take a bubble bath you are making an emotional deposit. You are ensuring that you will not get depressed when life sends trials. Calmness and clear thinking can be found whenever you make a withdrawal from your emotional bank account.

If you don't make regular deposits, you'll find yourself short tempered, difficult to get along with, making rash decisions along with suffering from headaches and upset stomachs. Not a pretty picture. *Is your emotional bank account empty or full?*

Emotional Bank

Start making deposits in your emotional bank account!

Energy

Some people will criticize you in an attempt to hold your back, rain on your parade, drain your energy. There is much written about this subject. For example, the person is unhappy, insecure, lonely, sleepy, etc. Take your pick. However, don't waste energy on their reasons.

Energy is a precious commodity. Use yours wisely. Sometimes you will not notice the subtle criticism until after the initial conversation. When you realize this, it's up to you to decide how to handle it. Taking action does not always involve direct communication with the person.

If it's someone that you want to continue to have a good relationship with, then you need to say, "I did not like what you said to me."

Then proceed to specify what you did not like. Open dialogue will maintain and grow your relationships. This may require a lot of energy, but this is a good investment.

However, if it is not someone in that category, then your job is easier. Limit your communications with this person to what is absolutely necessary. How you choose to use your energy is a personal decision.

Energy

Life presents enough energy zapping opportunities so you don't need to go out and look for extra ones. Of course, energy is meant to be dispensed, not wasted. Time is energy and energy is one of your natural resources. Use it wisely.

Everyone has energy. The quantity varies greatly from one person to the next person, but Mother Nature guarantees a certain amount to everyone.

Some people in your life will drain your energy and at times that is appropriate. A day as chaperone for five 12 year olds will definitely drain your energy. Driving nine hours to your family's home for the holidays is also an energy drain. These are all your choices and you accepted ahead of time that you would be tired.

Whether your job is teaching eighth grade English or cafeteria cook, you will be drained at the end of a day.

Look for energy generators, people or things that refuel your energy. There are many appropriate and necessary ways that you will use your energy for others, but do not neglect yourself. A nice bubble bath does wonders for mental and physical drain at the end of a day. I've heard some individuals say that they relax by watching their favorite TV sports program when they get home.

One universal regenerator is a good night's sleep. Rest is Mother Nature's way of refueling our tank. The number of hours varies from person to person and that is why it is so important to know yourself. Don't cheat because you will ultimately suffer and so will those around you. You are just as important as anyone else. Take time to evaluate how you use your energy. Write down where, how and with whom you spend your time. You will be surprised at what you have written and how you use your energy.

Writing things down usually make it easier to see things clearly. This process will allow you to pinpoint energy drains and productive energy usage. Some items you cannot change. Others you can. You will also discover your refueling stations.

I like my refueling stations. Sitting alone during lunch is refueling time for me. Listening to jazz music and doing Yoga exercises are refueling times for me and it's very relaxing. Reading my favorite books, newsletters or articles are another good source. You must relax to refuel, there is no other way.

We are all given 24 hours in a day. A major portion

is spent sleeping and working on a job that includes travel time. What will you do with the remaining hours?

Let's face it, no matter how much I surround myself with energy generators, every day I will have energy drains that are out of my control. Daily my energy is depleted and it will need to be replenished.

When you start your day, are you energized? If you are not, you are already in trouble. Waking up energized sets the pace for your day. If you are dragging, it's hard to catch up.

Maybe all you need is a good night's sleep. What ever the case may be, don't fill your days with too many activities. Leave room for incidentals. You do not want to be totally drained at the end of each day. There will always be incidentals. If you want energy, don't forget to regularly charge your battery. It's up to you. If you like dragging, then go right ahead and drag. *The choice is yours.*

Frustration

That financial investment did not produce the return you anticipated. What do you with frustration? The car stalled on a busy street during rush hour. The hot water heater burst while you were on vacation flooding your house.

Do not let it build into anger, stress, depression or even something worse. Know yourself. Watch for telltale signs, such as tight jaws, tense body and short, terse responses. Go outside, stick a pin in your hot air balloon and let the air out. You'll feel a lot better and so will everyone else around you. Take a deep breath, hold for a few seconds and blow it completely out. Repeat until you begin to relax.

Saying things out loud helps me put things in their proper perspective. This exercise does not miraculously take away the frustration, but it takes the steam away.

This puts a cap on it and prevents me from getting depressed. Try it. With patience you will notice that the frustration will begin to ease and disappear.

Everyone deals with frustration differently. Some withdraw or don't want to talk to anyone, even when a friend asks, "What's wrong?" Others get irritable, cranky or just plain difficult to get along with.

Frustration

We all have our moments. We all should allow each other that time and space to regroup. However two rules should apply. *#1 - while you are in that time and space, you do not have permission to be verbally abusive to others and #2 - others should give you time and space.*

Gas Tank

The next time you pull into a gas station notice how long it takes to fill an empty tank. Well, the same thing is true of your body. When your body's gas tank is empty, it will take longer to fill the tank up than if it were half empty.

Did you ever hear someone tell you to get a good night's sleep so that you will feel better tomorrow? If your tank is empty, it will take more than one good night's sleep. It may require several restful nights, plus a one-hour-vacation or two or three before you start to feel like yourself.

You want to make sure you get your tank completely filled, not half full. If you think you can start doing all the things you usually do with a half a tank of gas, you're wrong.   You are trying to go the distance without a full tank and you're surprised when you don't get there. Everyone runs out of gas now and then.

How often do you find your body's gas tank on empty? This is an important lesson. Don't let your tank get empty. You pay a very high emotional price for an empty gas tank. Your focus is blurred, you can't concentrate and your back aches. As you struggle to keep up the pace, everything seems to be coming at you all at once.

Gas Tank

No one can get inside of your body and determine when and how often you need to refuel. That lovely task is yours and yours alone. Your family and friends do care about you , but they have their hands full with their own gas tank. The special person you are just needs rest, not five minutes, but regular intervals of rest. *Do you know your body's rest intervals?*

Life's Track

I love going over to the local college track to take walks. Dozens and dozens of people go over to the track to walk each evening. Some walk for one lap, two, three or more laps. Then you have the people who walk ten or more laps. A few people walk with a partner or group.

I go over alone and walk at my own pace. One of the things I love most about walking is that everyone has their individual lane on the track. Even though there are several walkers in the same lane, we are so far apart that it seems you have a lane to yourself. Why is that? Well, each person walks or runs at their own pace. There is no competition. This is so refreshing. Society fills much of our lives with competition. It's good to be competition free.

From the moment we get up in the morning, it's a race against someone or something else. Usually we jockey for position from morning to night.

A typical day can start by competing for bathroom time with family members. Next is driving competition on the streets and freeways that lead to your job. Inevitably you want the same lane as many other drivers.

Have you ever had a morning where all the cars,

buses and trucks cleared a path for you?   Have you ever had a morning when you drove your entire route, at your own pace and without any interference? Of course not!

Then there's dinner.   I remember friends sharing stories about living in a household with eight, nine and ten kids. If you were not home by dinner time you may not get any food at all.   There were never any leftovers.   One friend even said, even if you were there, the biggest kids usually took what they wanted first. The other kids had to eat what was left-over.

Go to the grocery store and the search begins for the shortest check-out line.   Now let's think back to Thanksgiving when the markets had turkeys on sale. You get to the market and there's a crowd around that section.   You immediately start trying to get closer so you can choose your turkey and not be banished to slim pickings.

Another area where people often jockey for position is in the lives of their love ones. Small children will actually fight over who gets to sit on Mom's lap along with fighting to see who gets the seat next to dad at the dinner table.

As kids get older, they still compete, however, their

methods are more subtle. Sometimes kids pretend they are sick so they will get extra attention. One child may feel that Mom is spending more time with their other siblings. The daughter may feel that Dad is spending more time with her brother than with her. She may decide to tell Mom that her Dad doesn't love her any more. This usually gets his attention fast.

Spouses are very mature or maybe not about how they jockey for position. The husband states, ever so tactfully, that all of the wife's attention goes to the kids. The wife states, all of your attention is given to your job. Oh my, how direct, at least there's no guessing. Unfortunately some adults take a very long time before they directly ask for what they want. More competition.

When my two sons were small, they fought over who got to talk to me in the car. My oldest son, of course, sat in the front seat with me. My younger son sat in the in the back seat. I must admit, I usually enjoyed this opportunity for us to talk.

While merrily driving along I tried to stay relaxed because that is what drivers need to do. My oldest son and I talked about a variety of subjects and we would always get very engrossed in conversation.

My son in the back seat did not want to be left out. A funny thing would begin to happen. Whenever I'd forget this, he'd remind me by raising his voice to becomes part of the conversation..

Both sons starting competing with each other. They'd start talking louder and louder to make sure they were heard over each other. My youngest son is the funny one and he would get louder and louder and louder. They were times I thought I would lose my mind right there in the car.

Sometimes I would laugh and laugh and laugh. Other times I wanted to hurry and get to the destination because their raised voices, jockeying for my attention were getting on my nerves. Just writing about those times makes me laugh out loud. Oh, what great memories..............

Reserve Tank

Did you know that you have a reserve energy tank? Well, you do. Once your primary tank is empty, your body automatically switches to the reserve tank. If you are not paying close attention to yourself, you will not notice when the reserve tank is about to run out of gas. Just when you least expect it, you will look up and both tanks will be empty. If you think it takes a long time to fill up your primary tank, just imagine the time it takes to fill both tanks.

Too often I catch myself running on reserve. Both my mental and physical condition were dragging me along. Every part of me was hurting. Today I'm better at keeping my tanks filled than in the past, but occasionally I get caught with both tanks empty.

I know that I need to be careful about letting my energy get too low, but once again I wasn't paying attention. I had to push my body into the gas station.

What's in a gas tank? Fuel for life. Of course, you need fuel for energy. When both tanks are empty, you get headaches, backaches, short-temper aches, mind over-load aches, sleepless night aches, etc. The smallest infraction in your day seems like a major event. However more important is the lost of peace of mind.

Reserve Tank

When you are operating on fumes, your relationship with yourself and others will suffer. Fumes cause blurred vision, teary eyes, coughing and head aches. Other people should not have to take in your exhaust fumes. Monitor your tank continuously.

Notice when your behaviors and communications start to change for the worse. Negative self-talk is the beginning. Next you'll subject others to negative behavior and communication.

Rest is the only way to re-fuel your energy. *You don't want to look up one day, only to find your primary tank empty and you're operating on reserve.* Take some personal time off (go to the park or the beach, etc.).

Be good to your body and it will be good to you. Take care of yourself the way you take care of your family, your community, your job and everything else. Taking care of yourself is the prerequisite for taking care of the people and things in your life. This prerequisite provides the building blocks for healthy relationships. If not, you will become emotionally and/or physically ill.

Did you ever hear a parent tell their child, "Time out?" When a child gets loud, unruly, doesn't want to listen, parents will say, "Time out." They use this method to give their child time to calm down and think about what they just did. They tell their child to sit down and be quiet. Everyone knows this simple technique works wonders.

Time out works just as well for adults. Of course, you no longer have your parents to tell you when you when you need it. It's up to you to find a quiet corner, sit still and think about your behavior. Find one place or two or three to serve as your corner. No one will know what you are doing.

If you find yourself upset at work, try finding something to read that will take your mind off of what's upsetting you. If the telephone rings, it may be wise to let it go to voicemail.

For example, your mother has taken over your son's birthday party and you are getting very upset. With so many people around, you don't want to say the wrong thing, but you can go into the kitchen to give yourself a time out. Sometimes five minutes will give you a chance to think of how you want to handle the situation. You can hug her honestly and say, "Mom, thank you so much, I really appreciate all of your help."

For the next portion of the party, I have some specific plans, so I'll finish up the party. Hug her again and smile so she'll know you're sincere.

Time out has saved me many times from saying or doing something I'd regret. I don't always take a time out when I should. However, I have learned that regular time outs help me. It's an investment in me to benefit myself!

When you learn to pay attention to yourself, you'll realize, hey, it's time out again.

Not

Everyone

Will

Like

You

Benefit

It is so easy not to give a person the benefit of the doubt. When someone speaks sharply to you, assume they are preoccupied. It makes my day better if I think the best thoughts about a person. When I do not do this, it robs my plans for a good day, drains my energy and I can't allow that.

Think to yourself, the person actually spoke to me in a very pleasant tone. Some people are very miserable and they want to spread misery around. I refuse to accept their miserable message. Leave it with them. No, I don't always accomplish this, however most of the time I do.

I need all my energy for having a good day. I need all of my focus to be on what is working and not what I don't have control over. When I focus on what I can do, I find there are many, many things that I can do. There are really only a few things that I cannot do. If they are meant for me, they will eventually happen.

When my energy is low, I don't give the benefit of the doubt to others. How many times have you said to yourself, "I wish I'd given them the benefit of the doubt." A few things will kill your desire to do this. When you're hungry, tired or sleepy <u>you will not practice, "benefit of the doubt."</u> *For maximum benefit, Keep your energy high.*

Congratulations

Now, let's pretend that everyone likes you. What kind of life would you have?

There are six people in your office and each one of them likes you. Everyone exchanges gifts. They all give you birthday and Christmas gifts. Whenever they have barbecues, graduations or baby showers you are always invited. Therefore you have all these other obligations in addition to your own family.

For each person you automatically have two gifts to purchase yearly. Two times six equal twelve. Each barbecue means you have to bring a pot luck dish.

Okay, what else? Oh yes, graduations, baby showers, etc. That's another maybe twelve gifts' minimum. Here's the plan. Every January when you open a Christmas Club account, also open an account entitled "Everyone Likes Me." You will also have to give up some of your relaxation time to make sure you fulfill your "Everyone Likes Me" commitments.

Oh, did I forget some people? Let me think, now whom did I forget? Oh yes! Just to name a few others, such as, your spouse, children, parents, grand-parents and close family friends. Well, you are invited to every function and your calendar is completely filled each year.

Congratulations

Of course, you have the finances taken care of with your "Everyone Likes Me" account.

Now you have what you've always wanted. Aren't you really excited that everyone likes you? Your memoir will have many chapters devoted to all the functions that you attended.

Is this really what you want? *Congratulations!*

Will Everyone Like You, Ha Ha?

Do you think that if you are nice to everyone that they will like you? Ha Ha! Let me ask that again, do you think that if you are nice to everyone that everyone will like you? No, they will not. Ha! Ha! Hee! Hee! That's the way it is.

I was at a women's conference last year and something was said that I will always remember. I cannot see or hear very well, therefore I always sit in the front of the room. I like to use every method of communication available to me and non-verbal is one that I immensely enjoy.

As a motivational speaker, I know that usually the speaker's eyes are continuously scanning the audience. However, once in a while you'll lock onto someone's eyes for a few seconds. I was about to experience that as a conference attendee.

Traci had all of us in the palm of her hands. As she talked and walked about, I knew that we were speaking intimately to each other. I was revealing to her what I was thinking and she was the only person, of course, who could see my face and my body language.

Then Traci did something that I will always remember. She looked me straight in the eyes and said, "Everybody will not like you." I almost jumped out of my seat. I said with my facial expression, " Of course you are correct, so why do I keep trying?" *I guess I am a slow learner.*

Those five little words were why I was at the conference. When I remember something that someone said, it is a miracle because I cannot remember much. Some of my memory brain cells are missing. *Everybody will not like you.............*

Things Are Seldom What They Seem

Another family tragedy; Peter and Grace were getting a divorce. Both were well known in social circles. Therefore, everyone in the community was trading stories about their breakup. People were lining up and choosing sides.

The husband was a handsome, charismatic and successful businessman. He had a reputation for being arrogant, flamboyant and especially for doing things his way. Therefore, he did not have anyone on his side. People assumed he was the cause of the divorce. Story was that he had a girlfriend.

His wife was having an affair. He had decided to accept the affair hoping it would end. When the affair continued for years, he asked her to end the affair, but she refused. It was at this point that he decided to ask for a divorce.

Years later, he said, it was easier for his children to think that he was the bad guy. He knew that it would be terribly hurtful to them if they knew that their mother had been cheating on him for years.

We sometimes look at a person or a situation and with little bits of information jump to some pretty big conclusions. *Things are not always what they seem.*

You

Don't

Have

To

Stay

Between

The

Lines

Adopt

Most people think of children when they think of adoption. I adopt adults whom I support and encourage. I did not have to fill out adoption papers, pay legal fees or wait for approval. I simply say to myself, I want to adopt this person and it is done.

It's so easy; anyone can do it. For example, call the person's office voice mail at night and say, "Good morning, have a wonderful day." Everyone can use a nice message to start their day.

You can personalize your message depending on your relationship with the person, such as, "Thank you for being my friend."

Don't adopt someone that you already know well and spend time with because you already encourage them. Reach out to others. Everyone appreciates a, "just called to say hello and I hope this message finds you doing well."

There will be occasions when these words will make the difference between despair and hope. How many times have you asked yourself, "How can I help my friend?" It's easy. Pick up the telephone and leave a message. It doesn't cost a cent...

Send a greeting card for no special occasion. A person is guaranteed to lose ten pounds of anxiety upon receipt of the card. Write a personal note, such as, "I'm in your corner."

These kinds of messages are priceless. You can make a tremendous difference in someone's life. Before you know it, you will adopt one person and then a second and a third. *Do yourself a favor and start adopting today.*

Alberta Hunter

Alberta Hunter decided that she wanted to change careers and as usual she did just that. However, I think I should start from the beginning of her career. At the age of eight she sang for the first time in Chicago for $6 a week. She was hooked and decided that's what she wanted to do.

By 1912 at the age of 16, she began her official singing career known as the "Southside Sweetheart." Alberta rolled out with the handsome wage of $17.50 a week. She composed her blues songs, but couldn't read or write music. Alberta was a favorite and soon found lots of work in New York. She became a star on Broadway.

Broadway wasn't enough for Alberta, so she ventured to Europe. By 1927 she was a star in France as a show girl and on stage in England with Paul Robeson in "Showboat." Alberta stayed in Europe because there she could find work. Even though Hollywood had work for actresses, work was not open to Black people.

She continued to develop and expand her talents. Soon she was performing in cabarets. Alberta traveled from Stockholm, Germany, to Cairo, Egypt and sang in seven languages.

In 1934 she sang with Cole Porter and in 1935 made

her way into motion pictures. Radio was her next venue which she took by storm. Alberta performed on both radio and Broadway for several years.

Entertainment jobs dried up during World War II. At the young age of 50 she knew she still had some thing more to give, so she joined the USO and did seven tours.

Ms. Hunter continued adding impressive venues, such as, the Royal Theatre in London and Casino de Paree in Paris, France.

Now back to the beginning of my story, Ms. Hunter had accomplished all that she could dream in show business and decided she wanted a complete change. Alberta chose nursing as her next career and threw herself into that just as she had all her previous careers. Ms. Hunter proceeded to enroll in nursing school. She was a little confused about the instructions on the application regarding age.

The instructions meant that the maximum age to enroll was 40, but she was actually 60. Through the confusion, she put her age as 40. Undaunted, she completed nursing school and devoted herself to nursing. She did not perform in show business during her nursing career. Alberta never looked back. She enjoyed nursing and retired after 20 years (1957-1977). The hospital thought she was retiring at the age of 62, however she was actually 82 years old.

After retirement, Ms. Hunter did not have much to do, so she decided to start singing again. She found the public's appetite for music had changed quite a bit. She did however find a few small venues to sing the blues. It did not take her long to say yes and she picked up right where she left off in the late 1950's.
She returned to Paris, London and was even invited to sing at the While House for President Carter. She continued to entertain the world with her unique talents as a blues singer and performer until her health began to fail in 1984. Ms. Hunter died the same year at the age of 89.

Alberta was a woman for all times. A woman who didn't stay between any designated lines. She drew her own lines and in doing so, left a legacy for all. *Are you the designator of your life?*

It has been well over 2 years since I've worn a wrist watch. It seems incredible that I stopped wearing a watch and I don't miss it one bit. The story goes like this. I needed to replace the battery in my watch and finally did that. Little did I know the battery was bad. It only worked for a month.

Once again I had to remember to take the watch into a shop to get another battery. Finally, I remembered to take the watch to the shop. Little good that did me, the store was out of stock for that particular battery. Instead I purchased a new watch band to replace the torn one. Now I had a new watch band but no battery. Furthermore, upon closer examination, I did not like the watch band. It was a very cheap imitation leather.

As time went on, I realized that the absence of a watch really made no difference in my life. There is a clock in my car, clocks all over the house and one on my computer at work and home. Occasionally when I was out shopping and needed to know the time, I looked at my cell phone.

It has been over two years and I am now accustomed to not wearing a watch. One day I may decide to wear a watch again, but I know I don't need one.

Since I gave up my watch, I noticed that my pager

was another object that I had to carry in my purse. Continuing in this vein, I examined the contents of my purse, concluding that the load was still too heavy. The decision came easily, I did not need a pager either. Another clutter item eliminated!

Many times life points out the clutter to us, but it still remains for us to make a choice. Now that wearing a watch is history, it's one less thing I have to remember to put on, one less thing that I have to maintain and one less thing that I have to watch.

If you have a watch and you do not need it, don't wear it. If you don't have a toaster and don't eat toast, get rid of it. One less thing to clean because eventually the outside of the toaster will get grimy and need to be cleaned. If you have more magazines than you can dust, give them away. Others will be glad to read them, especially since they did not have to pay for them. Less clutter, less dusting.

If you have 100 pairs of shoes and have not worn 75 of them of in years, give them away. You notice I said give them away, not throw them away. Maybe you want to have a garage sale, if so, do it. Someone can always use what you have. Just imagine how much less clutter you will have, not just in your house but in your life.

Clutter

Then there is that big tree in your front yard that constantly drop leaves that you have to rake. At one time you loved that tree, but your life has changed. The kids are grown and you are out in the evening and weekends doing things that you enjoy. Even if you have a gardener, the gardener is not there every day to rake the leaves. Get rid of the tree or accept the raking with grace, the choice is yours.

Select how you want to fill your life. When you do this, you will realize there are many things that clutter your life and take your time. I periodically examine my life and look for new clutter that has <u>moved in</u>.

Is there clutter in your life? Identify it! Don't stop there. *Now, have a good time clearing the clutter.*

Computer

My computer and I are good friends. Some people may find this a little strange, however I don't understand why. I sit in front of my computer most of the day. Who else is closer, you guessed it, my PC. There is no logical reason why I should not talk to my computer. For instance, I might ask, "Where is that file I saved last week?" Now, understand, I do not get a verbal response, but it's better to talk to my computer and get the thoughts out. This process helps me find solutions.

Remember talking to someone every time you have a question or you need to talk can waste valuable time. It requires a lot more time explaining to a person than to my computer. My computer understands me.

I decided to start an on-line club, "We Talk To Our Computers." It's always comforting to know other people that you have something in common with. If you can't find a club to meet your criteria, *start your own.*

Get Away

My first weekend at the Ritz Carlton has been more than I ever imagined. I must do this again next weekend. I have written more over this Martin Luther King Jr. holiday (2000) weekend than any other single period. It's great and I feel very good about the material.

Let me tell you what I did. I told everyone that I was going out of town for the next three weekends. I needed to have some seclusion so I could write without interruptions from my own life. It's easy to let telephone calls go to voice mail and to stay inside of the house. However it is a lot more difficult to put your family and your household responsibilities on hold.

Then it occurred to me that my family room is a great place to get away. I told my son what I was doing and he smiled as he usually does at my ideas. Now that he is 18, I can make this arrangement. No pager, telephone or cell phone. I did not retrieve any messages.

My family room does not have a door, therefore, I had to improvise. And improvise I did. I took a sheet and nailed it to the door opening. Now I was set. I had everything I needed, desktop computer, lap top, color printer and of course, music.

Get Away

Eating was not a problem because the kitchen was only a few steps away. I told my son he could not reach me unless it was an emergency, which he liked. He thinks it's great when I am not home because I can't ask him to do any chores.

These periods of isolation proved to be very fruitful for me to write. You may want a rest from your regular routine or need solitude to make a decision. Whatever the reason, just do it. If you are not physically out of town, you can mentally be out of town. Do you have a Ritz Carlton? If you don't, there's no time like the present to create one. This was my secret until the publication of this book. Now that you know my secret, I hope you are planning a get-away. *You are where you think you are.*

Honey Do

What I have found out is I don't need to have my "honey, do list" on my mind. What's a "honey, do list"? Glad you asked. Well, it's a list usually prepared by a wife for her husband.

I have always heard guys talking about their "honey do list" which their wives give them and I realized that each week I, too, prepare a "honey, do list." So I started calling my list, "honey, do list." The only difference of course, is that I do not have a husband to give my list to. I'm the kind of girl who does what needs to be done, so I make out the list and give it to myself.

It's fun to hear myself say, my "honey, do list". It took a while for me to figure out that I don't need to try to do what two people can do. Decide what things are important and do just those things. If you like hot water and heat in the winter, pay your gas bill. If you like driving instead of walking, pay your car note. If you like to eat, go grocery shopping. If you like clean sheets, wash them.

On the other hand, if the kitchen floor is a little sticky and that does not bother you, don't mop. If you are out of toothpaste and you don't mind brushing your teeth with baking soda, don't add this to your list. If you don't see any reason to vacuum, don't.

Honey Do

If the drip-drip of the bathroom faucet isn't driving you crazy, don't change the washer. If driving a car that screams, "wash me, wash me" does not embarrass you, then don't wash your car. If the leaves accumulating in the front yard remind you of autumn in New York, don't rake the leaves. *It's your list.*

Nell

I've seen Nell twice and it will always be one of my favorites. I adore Jodie Foster, she always chooses excellent roles. DVDs were made for me because I rarely go to the movie theater. While I was watching the movie video, I kept thinking, "I can relate."

I wonder if people realize that we don't all hear music the same way, some hear notes between the notes. Oh, yes, the ones who know this are the ones who hear the notes between the notes. Nell had not spoken to any human being except her mother. The world felt sorry for her; an adult with the mind of a small child, so they thought!

Nell was discovered alone and frightened after her mother died. Nell's vocal cords worked very well.
No one could understand what she was saying. The authorities requested a psychological evaluation to determine her ability to take care of herself.

Almost immediately it occurred to me that living in a isolated cabin up in the mountains was not such a bad place to live. Nell had huge trees and her own private lake surrounding her home.

The initial evaluator assigned to determine her mental competence, did not take her away from her home. He spent a lot of time with her, discovering over a period of time that she was very intelligent. He also learned to interpret her language.

After spending a lot of time with her on her mountain he discovered something very amazing. Nell spoke English.   Her English was distorted because she learned to speak from her mother who suffered a stroke. She spoke with the same speak impediment as her mother.

The authorities convinced her evaluator that she belonged in an institution. She would make a prize case study. He gave in and brought her into the city. Next, she was placed in a tiny sterile room with a very large observation window. One researcher commented, "We have never had a patient like this." We have everything she needs here. Nell was so traumatized; she withdrew totally and stopped communicating.

Respect each other's right to be an individual and learn from the differences. We don't need to speak the same language or wear the same clothes to appreciate the Nells' of the world. When the music is playing, some people hear notes between the notes. There is no reason why everyone cannot be who they are. Her evaluator took her back home.

Personal Time

You need to spend time getting to know who you are, not who others say you are. When you invest in yourself, you will embark on a wonderful journey of self discovery. Learn what helps you maintain your sanity. Learn how you can walk in your own shoes.

If Saturday morning is your favorite time, then it's up to you to ensure that time for yourself. Others may try to interrupt your time, however it's your choice.

You have to take a strong stand when it comes to protecting your personal time. If you do not, then you will not have any. There will be times when you cannot control your time. One definite example is when you have young children. They wake up early and head directly for your room.

When the kids get older, many Saturdays are dedicated to extracurricular activities. However, you still need periods of personal time, even if it's only in increments of moments. It is harder to achieve when you have children, but it can be done. It's up to you......

One way is to wake up 30 minutes earlier than the rest of the household. Use this time for whatever you want. You may want to soak in a tub of your favorite bubble bath. If you are the type who just cannot get up any earlier than you have to, then you might try going for a walk at lunch time.

Another way, would be to sit in your car at lunch time, just be still and take a twenty minute nap. You will be surprised how that can rejuvenate your mind and body.

The only way you will know what works for you is to try several different ways to get your personal time. Personal time is extremely important. *If you do not get it, it's because you did not make it happen.*

Sack Full of Dreams

One day while listening to the song, "Sack Full of Dreams," it occurred to me that I too have a sack full of dreams. My sack never gets lighter. It stays the same because I continually dream.

I love to dream! My dreams have been my constant companion, my hope, my inspiration and my best friend. I have never opened this sack full of dreams and shared all of the contents with anyone.

Be careful whom you share your dreams with. Few people will give you encouragement, a helping hand, or support. Therefore be very cautious. When you have a sack full of dreams, you must be able to motivate yourself. *The last thing you need is direct or <u>insinuated</u> negative feedback.*

There are many ways to keep you inspired. Read books and magazines about people who made their dreams come true.

Join organizations and clubs to be around people who share similar interests.

I find that sharing dreams with others who have dreams of their own, is very invigorating. To watch someone's face light up when I talk about dreams is a joy!

Children, also need to have dreams. Share your dreams with your kids. Let them know that dreams do come true. The best example is one of your own dreams that came true.

Read them a book about people who are living their dream. Let them know early in their lives that they can choose a road that leads to dreams coming true.

You will find that encouraging your children or anyone else leads to *rekindling your dreams and creating new ones.*

When I die, my friends will talk about my dreams that came true. I have already given my friends' instructions for saying good bye when I die. They must have lots of laughs about the good times we shared. Talk about my dreams realized. Remember how hard I worked to live my dreams. Remember how much fun I had. Remember that I always had new dreams. I'll be listening.....

Socks

I love to walk around the house wearing socks and no shoes. Of course there was one problem with my relaxing technique. Every time I walked through the kitchen my socks would get dirty. When I noticed that my socks were dirty, I'd run and put on a pair of shoes.

It didn't take me long to realize the error of my thinking. When I corrected my thinking, I relaxed wearing socks and no shoes at home. The main reason for wearing only socks is to give my tired feet a rest. I am absolutely sure there aren't any shoes designed comfortable enough for my feet. My feet deserve a rest.

Once I changed my thinking, I saw things in an entirely different light, *my house, my socks....* Now, I realize that wearing socks helps to keep the kitchen floor clean.

When I walk over a sticky spot on the floor, it shows me the exact location to clean. It's all a matter of perception. My new theme is, "damage control." Furthermore, I have a dresser drawer full of socks that I no longer wear and this is a good way to get some use out of all the socks I purchased. Remember *this is a personal thing*, no one else cares if I walk around in socks or not.

Socks

Sometimes you have to change the way you look at a situation. By adjusting my perception regarding socks, I now completely enjoy the freedom. Have you forgotten the option of changing your perception? When faced with a situation, write down all the possible ways to look at it. Select the one that works best for you. Do you want to walk around in socks or do you want to paint your bedroom orange? It's your bedroom. Do you want to color your hair red? Even if the color is bright as a fire engine, it's your hair. What do you have to lose? If you don't like it, you can change it.

My feet thank me every time I walk around in socks. Your family and friends may not thank you for dying your hair red, but you'll be happy. There is no right answer, *only the answer's that's right for you.* Have you been playing it safe? Have you been staying between the lines of someone else's design? *You don't have to stay between the lines.*

Socks

Be free, change your perspective;
Is it music, cars, Uncle Henry, etc.?

Whatever it is, you can redirect your thinking.

Step Back

It's a conspiracy against women. I am sure of it. Have you ever noticed how bright the lights are in public women's restrooms? The lights are the brightest I have ever seen. One day I was in the restroom at work washing my hands. Unfortunately, I looked up and saw my face in the mirror and startled myself.

Even though I startled myself, I completed the task of washing my hands. Suddenly I came up with a solution.

If you are anything like I am, you don't want to leave the rest room thinking that you look awful. Not a problem, I have the solution. After washing your hands, take three steps back and look at yourself again. Oh boy, you look wonderful, great, fabulous. It's amazing what a difference three steps can make.

You're going crazy and beating yourself up about your bald head. You think being bald makes you look too old. You feed yourself negative thoughts about it. One day you are standing in front of the mirror and before you know it, you say out loud, I look so old. Your wife hears you, walks over, gives you a big hug and says your bald head make you look sexy. That's all you needed to hear. Are you standing to close? Step back and you see a sexy man.

Step Back

You're driving yourself insane over the five pounds you can't seem to shed. You assume that your husband thinks you are unattractive. He never said that but you feed yourself that negative thought.

One evening the two of you are getting ready to go out and you have changed clothes six times. You criticized yourself with each change. Your husband hears you complaining and he asks, "What's wrong?" You confess that you look awful since you gained five pounds. He thinks the weight that you've gained is in all the right places. *Take three steps back.*

You were driving yourself crazy trying to match the green in your favorite tablecloth. Stand back from it, and you will be surprised at what you see. From this view, you can see beige and two shades of peach. It will be easier to match the tablecloth now that you have more choices. Many times we are standing too close to a situation to see it clearly. If we can't see clearly, we definitely can't see the alternatives.

We each are made up of a complex tapestry of colors and shapes. The tapestry adds character and individuality to life. Life is like dance and poetry all movements and words are different. Take a look at yourself through fresh eyes.

Step Back

Stepping back allows you to see all of you, not the small unimportant things. Instead of focusing on perceived faults, you will see the *best of you*. Sometimes you may be standing too close to a situation to see the possibilities or appreciate what you have. *Take three steps back.*

Step Back

What areas of your life are you standing too close to?
Parents, children, friendships, business, or
Yourself!!!

Telephone

Unplug it. It's your choice. Between telephone solicitors and wrong numbers, I was going crazy.

About a year after the telephone company split the area code in my area, I started getting a lot of wrong numbers. It wasn't even the same person each time. This went on month after month. Finally I stopped answering my telephone.

I decided if the call was for me, the person would leave a message. I have the phone company's voice mail so I can't listen as the message as it is being recorded. When I did retrieve messages, there usually was no message. That confirmed it was another wrong number. Of course, if it was someone trying to reach me and they did not leave a message, I'll never know.

My newest toy was a telephone which displays the caller's telephone number. Next I decided when the phone rang, I'd look at the caller ID on my telephone. However some people have their number blocked or have an unlisted number. Why do people want their number blocked if they call someone? I don't even look at the caller ID anymore when the phone rings. I suppose famous people don't want their telephone number to get out to the general public. Other people may feel the same way. Telephone companies offer many options today and continue to come up with more such as, call waiting, call forwarding and a few others that are very useful. However, the caller ID blocking is the one that I do not like. If I place a call to anyone, I certainly have no reason to block my number.

When I get home from work, I immediately check phone messages. Very often I find that I received up to six calls but zero messages. During the evening the telephone rings several times and I'd answer, but too many of the calls were wrong numbers or solicitors. Everyone wants to sell me something.

Time to make another decision. I already crossed over a line that I never thought I would. When my kids were growing up, I always answered the telephone. I would never take a chance that the phone call was from one of them.

Pretty soon, just the ringing of the telephone was driving me crazy. It was yet time for another decision. I turned the ringer off. Now it's so nice not to hear the telephone ring. This is so cool.........

Once in a while I answered the phone. Telemarketers are trying to earn a living like everyone else so I don't hang up in their face. I listen for the 60 second introduction and then I say, "Thank you so much for the offer, but I am not interested and hang up."

Telephone

In the beginning, telephone marketers only called in the evening Monday through Friday. Another flash. They have updated their strategy to avoid disturbing people during dinner. They went from calling between 6 and 7 p.m. to calling after 8 and before 9 p.m. It doesn't end there. Apparently this still ticked people off. The latest development in telemarketing is Saturday calls. I answered my telephone last Saturday and someone wanted to sell me life insurance.

Something to consider, when the telephone was invented, it was supposed to be an asset not a liability. It should be an assistant not the boss. Does the telephone control you? The telephone was invented to be your assistant not the other way around. *Are you more productive or more anxious?*

Vacation

Design your own vacation. A vacation is for rest and relaxation (R&R). Below is a recipe for a one hour vacation. You can extend the time for as long as you wish.

> <u>1 hour vacation</u>
> 1 large beach umbrella
> 1 bright color blanket
> your best bathing suit
> sun glasses
> beach chair
> picnic basket
> cool refreshing drink
> music of your choice
> a book of your choice
> telephone off
> turn off all noise makers

Put on your best bathing suit, sunglasses, spread blanket on floor and put up umbrella. Next turn on your favorite music, open picnic basket, place cool drink at your finger tip. The most important step is to, sit down, open book, read, eat, drink and vacation. *Recipe can be customized.*

After your birth, your body was measured and weighed, followed by the ceremonial umbilical cord cut. You were given a name that was stenciled on your wristband.

The best is yet to come. Soon you'll be photograph ready dressed in a hospital issue T-shirt and diaper. The procedure is almost complete. Finally, your body is wrapped tightly in a small blanket. This particular wrapping technique is meant to simulate being in your mother's womb. Of course, you are not fooled.......

During the first 18 months of your life, your crib was in your parents' bedroom. However, your residence has been shifted into a bedroom with two older sisters.

You shared one bathroom with your mother, father, two sisters, two brothers and one grandfather. All of the bath towels were blue. The dishes were white and the glasses were a menagerie of jars and glasses with flowers. Some had no pictures and for sure no two looked alike.

How many years did you spend in that household? A game of Monopoly was allowed only after homework was finished and chores were done.

The living room of your parents' house had a sofa and love seat with bold flower prints and lots of oak wood. They each drove white cars. Your school uniform was a white shirt, gray pants, blue sweater and burgundy jacket. Every life detail was defined for you. You had to stay within the lines.

Lines were draw for you beginning at birth. That was then and this is now. As an adult, there is no reason you have to stay within the lines. You can move the lines of your life as many times as you wish. Towels can be purchased in purple, orange or pink. The furniture store carries a wide variety of colors and styles. You can draw your own lines.

For years Melissa had voiced consistent dissatisfaction with her job. There is nothing unusual about this. She has plenty of company. Little did she know that soon her destiny would arrive?

Fascination and passion came about while accompanying a friend on his truck route. After several months he let her take the wheel of his big rig on isolated roads. Before she knew it she found a new love, driving an 18 wheeler.

Melissa enrolled in trucking school to learn to drive an 18 wheeler. She completed the training, graduated and got her license. Soon she gave her employer a letter of resignation.

Melissa worked 20 years in an office job and wanted a change for many years, but didn't know what she wanted to do. All of her friends and family thought she was making a big mistake diving into a totally new world. Melissa had the courage to follow her own vision and never looked back. *You don't have to stay within the lines.*

Do Not

Let Your

Limitations

Limit You

Dad and Mom

I remember having a great time working with four guys, Howard, Craig, Jerry and Melvin. These four guys were always willing to talk to me about being a parent. Even when our conversations were not specific to parenting, their lives provided excellent role models. As a single mom raising two sons I had lots of questions.

When I started working with them, my sons were two and ten. During this time, one or more of these guys provided insights and practical advice. For the seven years we worked together, they were a tremendous inspiration to me. The single most important thing I saw in these guys was their *dedication to their own children.*

Howard loved to share childhood stories about him and his brother. He was the inventor of the phase, "Don't sweat it, it's not important." He had a way of telling a story which made me laugh and laugh.

One day he was telling me how much he loved basketball. He didn't want to give up playing basketball because he was a single dad raising a daughter. The solution of course was to take her with him. I could just imagine Howard playing basketball with his daughter watching nearby.

As with most children, she wanted to play too. He

taught her to play and she grew to love the game as much as he did. *Like father, like daughter!*

On many occasions, Melvin talked about being an only child. He said he heard lots of stories about sisters and brothers blaming each other when something was broken in the house. Each child would tell their parents that it was the other sibling who broke the lamp or spilled soda on the carpet. He said his mother did not have to ask who broke the lamp. *There was no one else he could blame.*

I especially admired Melvin because he took on the responsibility of single parent to his two daughters. He knew that they needed him and he became Mom and Dad. I often laughed imagining what their hair looked liked when they went to school. *How important is perfectly combed hair? Not important at all.*

On several different occasions, I'd be at the library helping my two sons with their book reports and Jerry would be doing the same with his two sons. He was showing them how to research and write a school paper. There was never a time that I did not know how much he loved his sons. He provided his sons moral support and practical instructions for their future. He wanted them to be all they could be.

Craig has two sons and one daughter. I remember

once asking him if his sons ever went through a stage where they were bullied at school. He replied, "yes." I explained that my oldest son was being bullied at school and I needed some advice. I further explained that when I listened to my son, I felt helpless. Craig said I was doing a great job as a parent and the most important thing I could do was to continue listening to my son. I told him I wanted to do more than listen.

Craig took the time to share a story about one of his sons. His son came home day after day unsettled by a class bully. He did a lot of listening to reassure his son that he understood his feelings. Craig also enrolled his son in a Karate class to help build his confidence. I could not find a class in my area.

Craig said that this stage would pass. I spent many hours listening to my son share his feelings. This seems like a lifetime ago, but I remember it like it was yesterday.

Melvin and Howard were the two clowns of the group. Craig was a little more serious and Jerry loved to have debates with me.

Those were wonderful times.

Dad and Mom

I am sure that they do not realize how I remember those days. None of these four guys said to me, "I love my children." They also did not have to say, "I will do everything in my power to support my children." They did not have to say anything, their actions spoke volumes.

All four of these guys made a positive contribution to my parenting life at a very crucial period. They told me I was doing a great job as a Dad and Mom.

You may not be able to find one particular person to be your *answer man*, but maybe one, two, three or maybe even four as I did. Look around and you will find resources that you can tap into.

I did not ask my girlfriends' questions about raising my sons because the best possible input could only come from men I respected. I wanted the best guidance and girlfriends could not provide firsthand experience.

What I needed I found in my four male co-workers. *Thanks guys.*

Do It Your Way

Do you hate hearing the alarm clock go off in the morning? Here's a few things to consider. Wake up to music or a recorded message of your own choosing. If you like the smell of fresh brewed coffee in the morning, buy a coffee pot with a timer. Let's face it, you have to get up in the morning. *Do it your way.*

I wanted to have flowers on my front porch and was determined to find a way. Finally I found two lovely planters that look very nice on the porch. Next I purchased my flowers, planted them and was thoroughly pleased with the results.

Not soon thereafter, I encountered a problem. I noticed that the flowers nearest direct sun were beginning to burn up in spite of being watered daily. This happened for the next two years. I, of course, experimented with different flowers, but the result was the same.

There had to be a way for me to enjoy flowers on my porch all year round without worrying the sun would burn them up. Brain storm! Why not put silk flowers in the planters. I bought some large beautiful lavender and beige flowers. I have a big grin on my face every time I drive up to my house. I did not need to water them or worry that the sun would burn them up.

I shared this idea with a very creative friend. Her negative response surprised me. She said, but the sun would fade the silk flowers. I replied, yes but not until I have enjoyed the flowers for many, many months. As usual I ignored my friend's comment. I enjoyed those beautiful silk flowers for two years before the colors began to fade. *There is always more than one way to do anything.*

At this point you may be thinking about something that you want to do or change. Be creative, if you are not, buy a book or magazine to guide you. Do it your way. *Exercise your options.*

Enjoy

I created a line of greeting cards because creating is what I do. I must create! I like to send greeting cards to my friends and there were many occasions that I could not find cards that conveyed what I wanted to say. Then it hit me. Why don't I make my own greeting cards?

Well I did not have any idea where to begin. Of course these are the times when I become absorbed in the challenge. I wrote words for the cards. Then, of course, I needed to design the cover. I looked for an artist to conceptualize my ideas, however I did not find one.

Not to fear, there is always a plan B, C and so forth. I decided to use free clip art from my computer and the Internet. After looking at hundreds and hundreds of samples, I managed to find three I liked.

Again I could not find exactly what I wanted but I moved on to the next step. I had a lot of fun in the process. I was excited and looked forward to each evening I spent working in my home office. There are many steps involved in bringing a project to completion and this one was no different. I learned about paper weight, paper finish, scored paper, etc. In the end my office was well stocked with a variety of paper.

Enjoy

I spent many hours preparing several different cards. When I could not find the paper size that I needed, I cut the paper myself. This proved to be a challenge, but the end result made me proud and I gained immeasurable experience. I was amazed at how many cards I had created.

I decided I needed to showcase my work in a portfolio. When all the cards were arranged in the portfolio, I was very pleased.

Does this mean that I found a way to market the cards on a large scale? No it does not. I was enjoying myself immensely. For a few months, I sold cards to friends and at craft shows. This gave me a great since of accomplishment. I also designed bookmarks and custom cards.

The more I created, the more creative I became. I already knew that I was creative, but this time I was even surprising myself. Some friends thought that I wanted to go into the greeting card business. I did look into that venture, but soon there was another project on my mind, *Writing a book!!!* The designs will always be there whenever I wanted to return to them.

I continue to write because I enjoy writing. *Joy at my finger tips!* God is the only one who knows the next sentence I will write, the next greeting card, the next bookmark, the next book or quote.

Guess what? *He did not send me an advance copy of my life.*

Writing about my perspective, my ideas is my thing. What's your thing? Is it cooking, car restoration, costume design, gardening, bowling or something else. *Whatever it is, do it today.*

Flowers

You like flowers and you wait and wait and wait for someone to send you flowers. Stop waiting! Send them to yourself. Imagine the smile on your face when the florist rings your door bell and says, "I have a delivery for........."

If you can't afford a florist, buy them from your local grocery store. You can choose from several beautiful arrangements and the price is very reasonable.

Look in your yard. You may be surprised to find beautiful flowers that you never noticed before. Put them in your best crystal vase. Stop saving that crystal for a special occasion because *you are a special occasion.*

If you don't have a vase, create one. Look for any kind of jar from the kitchen, wrap it with gift paper and tie a ribbon around it. Remember that old scarf that you like but no longer wear? That scarf will decorate any jar nicely. Now you have an original vase. *Enjoy your flowers.*

Let Go

Each person is unique and each day is unique. When you accept this as fact, you will begin to relax. When you relax, you'll enjoy each day. Each day will bring challenges, however, it will always bring pleasant surprises. Seek those pleasant surprises and let go of the rest.

Do you ever find yourself holding on to dumb stuff? You're 37 and you are still angry at Mary Ann for stealing your boyfriend in the 10th grade. Did she really steal him? Let go!

Your boss ripped apart your report in a meeting two years ago and you still want revenge. Use your energy for something positive. Let go! Your parents never attended your school plays or read bed time stories to you and it still hurts. Make sure you don't repeat that pattern with your own children. Let go!!!!

Your mother abandoned you at birth; you don't know who she is or where she is. You want to face her, ask her questions and let her feel your pain. Don't spoil the happy life you have with that anger. Let go!!!!

Letting go of things does not mean you forget them. If an incident causes you great pain or you can't seem to let go, seek professional help. It's important to let go so you can move past the incident and live a full life.

You can have a successful career, own several homes, travel the world and possess a seven figure portfolio and not live a rich life. No one other than you yourself knows if your heart is sad. The choice is yours, *store an experience in the back or the front seat of your life.*

Loretta Clairborne

She is a woman I greatly admire. Loretta over came many obstacles in her life which began for her at a very early age. She was born with partial blindness and an intellectual disability. Loretta was teased my classmates who said she was dumb and she couldn't do anything right.

Loretta continued to endure taunting and teasing. When she began to run track, she discovered something she could do well. She found her voice in the world and the love of her life. When she was running, she was free as a bird and it didn't matter if she was at the top of her class academically. She continued to practice and practice and eventually participated in many marathons. Loretta was soaring with the eagles...........

As her reputation grew, she became famous. I love the story of her turning down an opportunity to run with President Clinton. She already had a previous engagement to watch a musician friend play at an event. It was far more important for her not to disappoint her friend than to run with the President of the United States.

Loretta's life is truly an example of perseverance, determination and guts. We are all handicapped in some way. Take a lesson from her. Don't let your

Loretta Clairborne

handicap stop you from doing what you can do. She was born with her disability. What is our excuse? The rest of us picked up our handicap along the way. And just like we picked it up, *we can drop it off.*

Memories

When life stresses build up, take a *memory vacation.* The sole purpose of a memory vacation is to be bring you rest and recuperation (R&R). Healthy memories are in our span of control.

Don't be afraid of the dark memories because they did happen. Bringing forth bright, happy memories on a regular basis helps to crowd out the dark ones. When dark ones come, it is also a reminder that they are in the past.

If there are a lot of dark memories from the past, that's okay. Start today to create as many happy memories as you can.

Memories are a store house of experiences that can bring sadness, fear, pain, disappointment, regret, embarrassment, etc. On the other hand happy memories bring us laughter, peace, joy, replenish our energy and most importantly, remind us of good times shared with family and friends.

You will find the dark memories don't make you as sad as they once did and they don't last as long. Some memories come back in fragments for your protection. The human brain is the most complex machine in the universe. *It's the ultimate computer, designed by God, the master designer; messed up by man.*

Memories

Some memories are so sad and painful that your natural defenses bring them back in small enough increments for you to handle.

Regretting something that you have said or done is part of life. I regret the times when I opened my big mouth before thinking. Getting my big foot out of my mouth is no easy task.

Yesterday within a span of a few hours, I put my foot in my mouth twice. I immediately recognized that fact. If those who know you hold one or two statements against you, there is nothing that you can do about that. It's important not to hold on to small stuff and move on. This is a check and balance for me. My internal signal said, I am out of balance and I need to get back. All I have to do is be quiet. Rest..............

Dark memories will show up from time to time but there will not be room for them to stay! Go to the beach, or a picnic, museum, baseball game, whatever you like. You just created a happy memory. The more happy memories you create, the less room there is for sad memories to come and takes over. Keep in mind the human brain does not forget anything. There are just many storage cabinets.

Practice indulging in happy memories. Since life is

Memories

full of situations out of your control, stay busy
creating happy memories. Practice becomes habit.
Practice for joy and peace.

Happy Memory

Select a happy memory
One small memory is all you need
Use a photography or souvenir from that memory
or paint a picture
Select a frame that reflects your smile
Frame your memory, hang it where you can see it
everyday
Enjoy for a lifetime

Step

I see in my mind what kind of person I want to be and I step into that mold. I believe it is very important for me to start my day with the overwhelming idea that I will have a good day. I may wake up with a monster sinus headache, but so what!

It does not matter, how I feel when I wake up. I want to feel good so I walk and talk like I do.. As the day goes on, I will step into having a good day. With each passing minute, I am moving into the happy day mold and have a great day.

My sinus headaches can last for days and weeks at a time. It is vital that I step into the mold of having a great day.

This does not mean that sometimes I don't go talk to a friend and tell them what's on my mind. As I speak the words, "I am not feeling too well", I am still stepping into where I want to be. If I did not know who I want to be and where I want to go, I will not get there.

I have spent a life time, moving toward who I want to be and will continue to do so. This is a job that I am enjoying.. Find out who you want to be and enjoy getting there. If you want to smell flowers, plant some, if you want to dance, dance at home for yourself. Volunteer at a local school if you enjoy reading to children. Don't let others define who you are. *Whoever you are, be that person.*

Village

Have you ever wondered why you are so tired each day? Have you said, "I can't take it any more?" Did you ever wish that you had an artistic person in the family when your kids school projects come around? What do you do when your kids' teacher tells them that they have one month to build a fort? Or maybe the assignment is to write about life in the 1930s. Wish you had a relative to interview who lived during this era to talk to your child instead of relying solely on hours of library research.

In a village, there is a historian and an artist. There is also a bread maker, a gardener, a cook, a financial planner and more. Whatever you need is in the village.

Of course, we no longer live in a village. I long for the village life. One of the reasons why people are so tired today is that they try to do everything and the frustration comes because they do not have the skills. Whenever I try to do everything, I drive myself nuts.

Even though we no longer live in a village, we can create a village concept. It takes only two people to start the concept. When you need help, call each other. Share your talents. Add a third person and a fourth. *The village can be any size, just do it.*

What If

Do you have a "what if list?" What if you were 5'1" tall? What if you had a 24" waist line? What if you had a Ph.D.? What if you still had hair on top of your now bald head? What if you could sing? Everyone seems to have a "what if list". Of course this list is not for public information. No one would admit they have a "what if list." It would be too embarrassing.

I definitely have a "what if list." What if I did not have big feet? What if I did not have bunions? What if I did not have allergies? What if I could drink all of the orange juice that I wanted? What if I had a college degree?

What if I could drink milk? What if I did not have sinus headaches? What if I could eat foods or drinks with citric acid, and a many other things?

Your list could look like this. What if my Mom did not walk out on my Dad when I was 10? What if my Mom and Dad were not alcoholics? What if I did not run away from home at 14? What if my brother didn't rape me? What if my teachers encouraged me? What if I were an "A" student?

What if kids did not laugh at me? What if I were 5' 5" tall instead of 6'5"? What if I didn't take that first drink when I was 12? What if my Father didn't beat me? What if my Mother loved me? What if my sister didn't call me stupid? What if I went to college after high school instead of getting married? What if I started a retirement saving plan when I was 21?

Apparently I do not need small feet to walk through this world.   Actually bunions remind me to be careful what type of shoes I buy. Allergies force me be very aware of what I eat and monitor my reaction. Milk may be good for some bodies, but my system does not agree.

I decided that a "what if list" is okay.   There is nothing I can do to make those things go away, so I make fun of them. I have had many laugh attacks regarding my list, so why not join me with your list?

Go ahead make your own personal "what if list" and join my laugh club. There is no membership fee and I promise not to mail you anything or call you. It's just for you to realize that in spite of your "what if list", you have a wonderful life. Did I hear someone say, "I do not have a wonderful life". My reply is, "why not?"

You Can Live

A Rich Life

Without Being

Rich

Cast A Wide Net

There are many people waiting to be caught in your net. Make it your life's work to be a fisher of men. Hopefully you will soon realize that every time you bless someone, you are blessed as well.

Cast a wide net, the more people you catch, the more you will be blessed.

Champion

I've heard that "every woman needs a champion". A person who will cherish her and support her every step of the way. I could not agree more. Every woman needs a champion, as well as every man, boy and girl. A champion listens, listens and listens.

Are you looking for safe place to share your concerns? When you want to celebrate your success, whom do you call? When disappointment knocks at your door you need more than a cup of coffee. You need a special friend.

Charles was up for a promotion. His credentials, education and experience far exceeded that of any of the other candidates. He also had a dozen letters of recommendation. Charles was a hard worker and had an excellent reputation with his company. Finally there is an announcement. It was not Charles. He needs a champion.

A champion acknowledges your pains and disappointments. A champion provides a safe haven to share these feelings. A champion wants the best for you and will do whatever they can to help you. . A champion does not interrupt you in the middle of a sentence to correct your subject and verb. *A champion provides an unlimited* supply of support, encouragement and most important of all, love.

Champion

When you are talking to your champion, you feel a certain bond that only happens in special relationships. I need more than one champion. I would drive one champion nuts! Since I need more than one champion, does anyone want to adopt me?

Do you have a champion? You may need to be your first champion because not everyone was raised in a championed environment. If you were, don't forget to say, "Thank You" while they can still hear the words. Champions are not perfect people. They are perfect as *your champion*.

Looking for a rewarding experience, become a "champion". There are so many people who would love to have someone in their corner. A *champion is someone who is always in your corner*.

Coffee Beans

Michelle is one of the millions who love coffee. She always wanted to buy coffee beans and have really fresh coffee. While at the grocery store, she found herself face to face with the coffee bean decanter. She said, this is it, I'm buying myself some coffee beans.

Michelle completed her shopping and headed home with her groceries. When she arrived home, she pulled the coffee pot down from the kitchen cabinet and proceeded to make her first pot of really fresh brewed coffee. After she put the coffee on to brew, she put the groceries away and anxiously anticipated her morning coffee.

She wondered off into another room and started her house cleaning. After a while, it occurred to her that the house was not filled with the aroma of coffee. Michelle decided to go into the kitchen and take a look. Much to her surprise, there wasn't any coffee in the pot, only water. She assumed that she did not put enough coffee in the pot so she added more.

Again she went about the house waiting for fresh coffee. More time passed and still no coffee aroma. Michelle returned to the kitchen again and saw the coffee pot filled with water. Not to be disappointed, again she poured the water into the coffee maker and added more coffee.

Coffee Beans

She again returned to her activities and forgot about the coffee. Her husband returns home in the meantime and asked her to come into the kitchen.

When she made her way to the kitchen, he asked, "what are you doing?" She replied, I'm making fresh coffee from coffee beans. Michelle explained how she continued adding coffee beans to the pot, hoping to get the coffee made. He said, you don't get coffee from coffee beans. He said, "you have to ground the coffee beans first and then put the grounds into the coffee pot."

Of course, I laughed so hard I was falling on the floor. I kept saying, you didn't put coffee beans in the coffee pot and expect to get coffee. She replied, "yes, I did."

How many of you have a great story like this one? *Share your stories and spread some EPA, FDA approved laughter.*

Dedicated to dreamers
and those who need encouragement
to become a dreamer.........

Dream A Dream

awake or asleep
the dream is the same
sitting or standing
the dream is the same
hungry or full
the dream remains
dream a dream

tired and sleepy
the dream does not rest
the winds blow
the earth shakes
still the dream stands
dream a dream

see it
feel it
say it
write it
sing it
Dream A Dream

2001 Shirley A. Smith

Library

The library has always been my friend. I've had a library card since I was five years old. Today I have three cards for different library systems. I march into any of those libraries and walk out with an armful of books. I can read one or all. I can extend the due date. I can take the first arm load back and check out another arm load of books. Libraries are wonderful.

Even before you begin taking your children to the library, their home is their first library. My children got their first book before they were old enough to talk. They were infants when I bought their first book. By creating your own home library, you'll set a legacy for generations to come.

As an adult I love books just as much as I did as a child. I also buy books. However if I get the book from the library and don't like it, I just take it back. I don't want to own every book I read. I can research any subject and request books from other libraries. *Aren't libraries great?*

Children automatically love books. Expose them to books at an early age and they will soak them up like a sponge. Books provide a *life time of fun and enrichment.*

Meaning

One thing that seems to be quite common is the search for meaning in an individual's life. You can read about it in many books, articles, see movies, go to seminars, conferences or just listen to someone talk about it. Looking at someone else's life can encourage you, inspire you but no one can do the work for you, that's a choice. *Find your meaning!*

What's the work? Good question! The work is spending time along with yourself, taking note of the things that you like to do, not forced, but natural. Find ways to spend more time doing those things You may say, nothing comes natural. Use other people's lives as a example, a starting place but you are not someone else, you are you. Create your own pattern. You are unique.

You are not Michael Jordan, Oprah Winfrey, Bill Gates, Tiger Woods, Albert Einstein, Mozart or Judith Krantz. You are not Jonathan the green thumb, Susan the story teller or Maria the cake decorator. These individuals found their way and their place.

Remember how much you enjoyed art while you were in elementary school and high school? Well, you never even thought of pursuing a career in that field and forgot all about it. Well, it doesn't matter what career you chose, go enroll in art classes for your personal pleasure and satisfaction. *Meaning is where you find yourself and that is different for each of us.*

Mother Hale found her meaning in helping children. When she was raising her own children, she raised other children as well. She found her meaning early in life and thus didn't have to search. I consider her very fortunate because she spent her life doing what she loved.

She later discovered another way to help children by giving her loving care to babies born suffering with drug withdrawal. She began with one baby, then another and another. Mother Hale couldn't refuse a baby. As time marched on her home began known as Hale House. She provided a home for babies suffering from drug withdrawal. What did she give them? Something that cannot be purchased or manufactured. She gave them her time and her warm safe loving arms.

Mother Hale held them against her chest and they felt the rhythm of her breathing. They were bathed with tender loving hands, dressed in clean clothes, wrapped in a warm blanket and given a bottle. The bottle fed their physical body, *but it was her love that fed their emotional body.*

Meaning

How did she do this? Next came the most vital part of their care, *she held them close.* The babies did not wonder where they were, they knew they were safe at home with their Mother Hale. As these babies suffered through drug withdrawals, she held them, rocked them and loved them. That's love, Mother Hale's style. Home is where the love is.

If those babies could speak, they'd say, we're home. She did not hold them for one day or two or three. She held them day after day, week after week and month after month. No doubt, these babies were cheated while they were in their mother's womb. Their mother's womb was supposed to be their first home, however Mother Hale gave them their first home. She gave them their first experience of being cared for. A woman who can hold a baby fighting the ravages of withdrawals, has meaning.

Mother Hale did not need others to support her mission or tell her this is what she should be doing. She just lived her life doing what she loved to do. *You have the same choice.*

It was an ordinary day. Nothing much seemed to be occurring until I read a story about a group of friends sharing their life's successes.

Kevin was a VP with his company of 25 years. His stock portfolio, restaurants and prime real estate holdings provided security for him and his family. He could retire and live very well for the rest of his life.

Tiffany was a real go-getter. She worked several part time jobs including her regular 9 to 5 and saved a large portion of her income. She invested in real estate and owns a very successful designer dress shop.

As the discussion continued, Mike proudly said that his 200K plus salary, bonuses and perks afford him everything he desired and more. Marva just opened her second hair salon and bought a new Mercedes.

Lois only flew first class and stayed at the most expensive hotels when she traveled. Her most recent trip was to Paris, France. She has her own law firm and sits on the board of directors for several fortune 500 companies.

Ava was retired. She was living the life of great comfort. Her home was paid for, allowing her peace of mind. Ava's monthly income from investments provided her many luxuries. Another example of success.

All of these success stories are wonderful and those individuals worked hard for their success. However, there are many types of success and many ways to measure success.

I admire those who are wealthy as well as those who are devoted parents and grandparents. Parents who nourish, support and guide their children into adulthood are the most important and successful individuals in the world.

Teachers have a major impact on the lives of children and their commitment to helping each child achieve is success at its best.

The school crossing guard is vital in assuring that children cross the street safely. Every day they are on the job, they are a success. Not everyone's schedule will allow them to be a school crossing guard but thank goodness there are those who can.

The person who raises fresh vegetables on a small patch in their back yard is a success. Not everyone can raise fresh vegetables. Some of us have a blue thumb instead of a green one.

Measure

There are books, tapes, conferences, college courses, etc., telling you how to be successful. Are you a success? Do you want to be a success? Have you ever thought about being a success? Most people don't think about being a success. Few families and/or schools use the word success.

Success is usually implied. How is it implied? When babies take their first step, parents don't say, "*whoopi you're a success*". They say things like, "that's my baby" or "look at my baby". When first graders bring home a class drawings or any school assignment, it is immediately placed on the *wall of fame*, the family refrigerator. In others words, we learn what success means by what others think of what we do.

Another way to look at this. We learn that success is measured by everyone else but ourselves. Do you wait for someone to tell you that you are a success? Are you still trying to please your parents, employer, family and friends. *Because if you are, you will continue to be held prisoner waiting to be released by their affirmations.* The more power you give others over your life, the more they will use it.

If you allow others to measure your success they will. Not only that, each will use a different measuring device. They may judge your success based on such things as social standing, position with your company, zip code or the balance in your treasury account. Success is not solid, you can't hold it in your hand, so how do you measure it? *Whenever you accomplish something that makes you feel good, you are a success.*

Measure your successes with a personal scale. Give yourself a raise! Raise your confidence! Raise your potential. Raise yourself from depressing thoughts. Raise your children to be successful human beings. *Raise yourself to live a rich life.* Don't hold back. Fill your wallets. *You are rich!*

Override

When the alarm clock goes off, what do you do?? You turn over; lay there another 15 minutes or more. When you finally do get up, you call a friend instead of getting ready for work. Each decision eats away at your getting ready for work time.

Override is something we all do many times each day. On your drive into work someone cuts you off in traffic nearly causing an accident. Just as you overrode the alarm clock before you left home, override your impulse to curse at them. You arrive at the office and you say good morning to a fellow co-worker, however they do not respond. Override the initial thought, how rude they are. Instead think, they are preoccupied.

The same way your override the alarm clock and getting ready for work, override your negative impulses. Use this technique to override jumping to conclusions or telling someone off.

This override system is for your personal benefit, peace of mind and blood pressure control. It takes practice to implement any new change in your behavior. Nothing works every time, but just imagine with practice how much more relaxed you will be each day. Do you want to increase your relaxation and decrease your agitation? *You already use override in your life, just expand it to include other situations.*

Passion

What is life without passion? What is skiing without passion, river rafting, sky diving, or sailing without passion. Sculptors, painters, dancers, writers, actors, and other creative people all have one thing in common, passion for their craft. I love being around passionate people.

I love with passion, hug with passion, speak with passion. I am passion driven. Find something that you are passionate about and watch the difference in your life. You will not have to say, I am passionate about gardening, *it will be apparent in your garden.* Your life's passion is reflected in your actions. *What is your life's passion?*

An example of this is my friend, Charles. He restores classic trucks. When talking to him, it's easy to hear the passion for his craft. He enters his trucks in many shows and travels with a group of his peers. What a beautiful sight whenever they drive down the street. People admire the trucks, but I wonder if they have any idea how much time and money it takes to lovingly restore one truck.

It requires a great deal of patience to search for original parts. Charles does not see the results of his restoration for years. From the first phase of the restoration to the last, he's focused on bringing back the truck's original beauty. The restoration is a painting that slowly becomes the masterpiece that the artist and the public will eventually admire.

Just as a painter sits down at his canvas and slowly develops a picture, so it is with truck restoration. Each phase reveals the picture already etched in his mind.   Passion keeps Charles focused until the restoration is complete.   *Passion.*

Martha found her passion for baking at an early age. The first cake she baked with her mother's assistance did not turn out like the picture in the cookbook. Martha knew she could do better, so she continued to bake cakes until the finished product looked like the picture in the cook book. Martha discovered that she loved the art of baking and enjoyed sharing her sweets with family and friends.

She next began creating her own recipes and baking for special occasions. She continued this through high school and decided she had found her career.
Her passion is now her career.   *Isn't Martha fortunate?* Sometimes it takes some of us longer than Martha to find our passion, but it's there. Some years ago, a friend and I were talking about our jobs. After listening to Sandie for a while, it became apparent that she loved her job.

Then she went on to correct me further. She said, this

Passion

is not a job, it's my career.

Sandie spoke with great passion about her Human Resources job. Oh, I mean career. She said she was doing what she wanted to do. A career is doing what you like and getting paid for it. I pondered this concept before replying. Finally I responded, *I have a job not a career.*" Of course this opened up a different conversation about a job verses a career. In the end I still said, "I have a job not a career."

I was glad that one of us had a career. She was doing what she chose to do. I was not. When Sandie asked me what I meant, I explained to her that I work 40 hours a week without having passion for what I am doing.

Have you ever tried to interest others in <u>your ideas</u> without passion. Of course, it doesn't work. Who are the top sales persons? The ones with passion. *Passion is persuasive. Passion is contagious.*

Some people have a passion for getting together with friends to watch a football game, play golf or play cards. When you discover your personal passion, you will want to latch on to it. If you have lost yours, track it down. Do whatever you need to do to regain it. If you think you don't have passion for anything, then get busy searching. *Passion is a main ingredient for a rich life.*

Later in my life I realized that I was living my passion. I like to help people by donating clothes, my time, talents and money to various organizations. It is a special passion to inspire and encourage women on their road back from substance abuse. I also rediscovered my passion for writing and thus an old love was rekindled and that flame continues to burn brightly. I am having a love affair with motivational speaking and writing. *What's your passion?*

Poof

Why I woke up at 4:00 a.m. with a story on my mind, I'll never know, but I was obedient to the call. I guess this story was priceless and I had to add it to this book.

It was an ordinary work day in my life. I got up at 5:30, oh let me be honest, 5:45 a.m.. I went to work and was having my usual fun filled day. I tried to stop it, but it happened anyway. It was lunch time. Lunch time provides an opportunity for me to be alone, be still and relax, but especially to *recharge my battery.*

Lately I had been bringing a sandwich for lunch so I could by pass going to the microwave. I like trying something different and this was a day for that.
Since I was tired of eating tuna sandwiches, I decided to try tuna with crackers. My lunch was in the refrigerator therefore I headed off to the canteen to retrieve it. As I removed my lunch from the refrigerator, I made an observation. It was very crowded in the canteen. Nearly every seat was taken.

My next thought was one of my truly unique *"brain storms"*, which I have occasionally. I thought to myself, "put the crackers in the microwave for a few seconds so they won't be cold." Self replied, "good idea." I proceeded to put the crackers in the microwave, close the door, set for 10 seconds and pushed start. I looked away for a second and suddenly I saw a flame out of the corner of my left eye coming from the microwave. Twas a big flame, a forest fire. I saw big trouble. *Poof!!* Instead of panicking and screaming, I grabbed a few paper towels, quickly opened the microwave and smothered the flame.

Five seconds still remained on the microwave timer. Apparently the microwave did not like the plastic wrap on the crackers. Fortunately, only a small portion of the plastic melted. The crackers were fine and I was no worse off for the experience. I came away with a very minor burn on one of my fingers.

My back was to the people sitting in the lunch room. I slowly turned around to see if anyone was watching me and no one saw a thing. I started laughing so hard I could barely contain myself. I laughed and laughed as I went out to my car. The office would have a field day with this one. I would have won the *booby prize*.

After lunch I called one of my friends. I was still thinking about the microwave and my crackers. As I was telling her the story about the big fire, I started laughing again. I could barely tell her the story. Before long I was laughing so loud, people in the office were looking my way and my boss came out of his office. I was doubled over and crying tears of laughter. *I was hysterical.*

I thought my story was funny and she agreed, however she said she had a story to top mine. Her story was good, too. Her story is included in this book; coffee beans.

Moral of this story, *stuff happens, enjoy it.*

Reading

I love reading. My reading history goes like this: best sellers, mysteries, plausible science fiction, adventure, detective and history. I've also read a few romance novels. My reading appetite changes over time.

Today books that encourage, inspire and fuel my creativity are by favorites. I like reading about real people making a difference in the world. Big on my list are books about people who live their dreams in spite of obstacles. I am drawn to their determination and focus.

So much of what I read is for information. I am overloaded with daily reading material. A certain amount of informational reading is necessary. It is important to keep up with local, national and world news. However, I always make time to read for pleasure.

I recently read two romance novels that I really enjoyed. Both had a happy ending and I definitely like that. One thing that I love about reading is all of the choices available to me.

If I start reading a book and I don't like it, I just don't complete it. Other people say if they start a book, they must finish it. I can start reading a book, put it down and never pick it up again.

Reading

Find something to read that does not drain you. Some people I know love cars, so they read car magazines. Whatever your interest, you can find books, magazines or the Internet to satisfy your reading appetite. Find something to read that makes you laugh, something that takes you on an adventure. Reading books are within everyone's reach. *Reach for a book today.*

Two 4 One

Everyone loves a bargain, a deal. Everyone loves to get something extra for their money or time. Go to the grocery store and a sign says, two bags of apples for the price of one. You automatically want two 4 one. Of course you might not have any need for that many apples, but the market is betting that you cannot resist. Restaurants use the same strategy. Buy one steak dinner and get the second one ½ price. It certainly draws more customers into the restaurant for dinner.

Go to a department store and see big signs which say, buy one suit and get the second one free. You may only need one suit, but the advertisement is irresistible. You walk out of the store with two suits instead of one.

My favorite example of two 4 one is with people. Quite by accident, I discovered something. Well, what did I discover? I'll tell you. I cannot encourage anyone without encouraging myself. The next time you need encouragement, find someone to encourage. Instantly you are also encouraged. Two 4 one.

If you are feeling anxious, out of sorts or depressed, encourage someone. It will not cost a cent, you will not have to stand in line, try on clothes or have two bags of

Two 4 One

apples rotting away in your refrigerator. Try this and your life will receive an immediate lift. *Two 4 one.*

DYING

Dying

Several months ago I spent 4 hours with a friend who was dying. Four hours that I will never forget. Four very special hours of sharing and it was done primarily without speaking. We were not best friends; we were friends through a mutual friend.

When I found out the chemotherapy was not successful I knew I wanted to go see her while she was able to hear me. The doctors had given her three weeks to live. Soon I would visit her laid out in a casket.

Several thoughts went through my mind before I called to see if I could visit her. She was at home because she did not want to die in a hospital. I was not sure what I would talk about. I was not sure if I would make her feel better or worse. The first thing I did was send her one of my poems.

Days later I telephoned her daughter and asked her to ask her mother if I could come for a visit. The answer was yes. I got the directions and drove over on that Saturday afternoon (Labor Day weekend 1999). I took a change of clothes with me because I was going to leave her house and go to a birthday party. It was my best friend's parents 80th and 83rd birthday. I did not want to miss the gala event.

When I reached the apartment about 4:30 p.m., there

was a sign on the front door saying, "Please limit you visit to a few minutes." I rang the doorbell. Her daughter answered the door. We said our hellos and hugged. I looked past her and saw her mother sitting in a recliner. I had not seen her mother since the cancer diagnosis.

When I looked at her, I saw that cancer had destroyed her body. Jeri opened her eyes to acknowledge my presence and then I saw it. Her eyes said to me, my spirit is 100% intact. Jeri smiled, we exchanged hellos and I hugged her. Jeri did not have the strength to hug me back! Her Mother was sitting next to her. She got up and let me sit in her seat next to the recliner.

One of her good friends was typing her obituary on the computer. She was giving instructions for her obituary. Jeri gave details about organizations she belonged to. Also she provided names of family members, etc. Jeri was taking care of every detail of her funeral.

She had picked out her burial dress and that was the only garment hanging in the closet. Before she became too ill, she had given away all of her personal belongings. No one would have that chore after her death.

Dying

She asked me what I had been up to and about my sons. Jeri talked for a few minutes and then she closed her eyes. She was very tired!

Every so often she'd open her eyes and say something to me. At one point she asked her daughter to put on a gospel cassette. She loved gospel music. We sang together on several songs. I will never forget sharing time with her. I don't have a good voice but nevertheless we sang beautifully together.

As I sat in the chair next to the recliner, I put my hand on her hand that was resting on the arm of the recliner. Most of the time I was there her eyes were closed. I did not know what to do, so I did what I know and that was touching her, I rested my hand on her hand.

When I thought she was asleep, she'd move her hand to reach for mine. She let me know she knew I was there. I cannot remember how the clock ticked away. I knew I was supposed to be gone. She had her mother and daughter to take care of her, but I could not seem to bring myself to leave.

Three other visitors came while I was there and they talked to her for a few minutes. Two of the three visitors was a mother and daughter.

Dying

They talked a few minutes and they left. A third visitor came and stayed for a few minutes. I moved out of the chair next to her so the new guest could sit next to her, but none of the 3 chose to. After that guest left, no other guest came that evening. Of course, I should have gone too.

I resumed my seat next to Jeri and laid my hand on top of her hand. I just wanted to touch her. I sat there until she wanted to say something. It did not matter to me if she ever spoke. I always thought she was asleep, but she said she did not sleep much. She was dying but that did not stop her from being herself.

At one point she moved her hand away from mine over to the buttons on her pajama top. I had no idea what she was trying to do. She very slowly pulled the pajama top up exposing her stomach. She had very little strength so everything she did was an effort. There was her stomach in the shape of a pouch. It looked as though she was four or five months pregnant.

Jeri previously weighed 170 lb. and now weighed only 80 pounds. She told me that the doctor told her that mass was all cancer. I reached over rubbed her stomach and she smiled. Jeri never explained why she wanted me to see her stomach and I did not ask.

Dying

We were speaking to each other without using words. It was another way for me to touch her. Later it occurred to me that maybe she just wanted me to see what the cancer had done or what my reaction would be. It didn't matter. *I am grateful that she trusted me enough to do it.* She smiled a lot during our visit.

Before I knew it, several hours had passed. I couldn't believe that I sat next to her that long resting my hand on top of her hand. Occasionally I'd rub her hand and she'd smile.

I looked at the clock and it was 8:30 p.m. Finally I knew I had to leave because her mother and daughter were tired and ready to go to bed. The note on the apartment door said, stay only a few minutes. It was hard to get up and leave. I wanted to hold her and hold her and hold her. I no longer had the heart for going to the birthday party. I left and went home.

When I got home, I was still in a state that I cannot describe. I wanted to keep the feeling of peace that Jeri and I shared. I wanted to remember our hours together so I decided to write this story. As I was writing, it occurred to me that the guests who came to visit never touched her. They also did not sit next to her.

Dying

I went back on Sunday about 3:30 p.m. but she was extremely weak and the family said to stay only 5 minutes. She opened her eyes and said, hi, but I could tell she did not have much longer to live. I was very grateful for the time we spent together on Saturday. She died two days later.

When I lay dying, *I want to be touched, don't you? When I lay dying, please touch me.*

A Few Of My Favorite Quotes

The world is a dangerous place to live in, not because of the people who do evil, but because of the people who let them.

> Albert Einstein

I cannot teach anybody anything; I can only make them think.

> Socrates

I have learned that success is to be measured not so much by the position that one has reached in life as by the obstacles which he has overcome while trying to succeed.

> Booker T. Washington

And we know that all things work together for good to them who love God, to them who are called according to his purpose.

> Romans 8:28

Love is the key and we each have one. Are you using your key?

> Shirley A. Smith

The ultimate measure of a man is not where he stands in moments of comfort and convenience, but where he stands at times of challenge and controversy.

> Martin Luther King Jr.

A Few Of My Favorite Books

The Bible

Their Eyes Were Watching God
   Zora N. Hurston

Live Your Dreams
   Les Brown

Grace for the moment
   Max Lucado

God Uses Cracked Pots
   Patsy Clairmont

Perfect Trust
   Charles Swindoll

Tuesdays With Morrie
   Mitch Albom

Journey through Heartsongs
   Mattie Stepanek

God's Little Devotional Book

Who Will Cry for the Little Boy
   Antwone Quenton Fisher

Peel

Dedicated to me…………………..and you too……

Peel

Peel

Peel

what you see

is it real

look a gain

did you peel

peel a way

the layers of

des pair

lon li ness

cau tion

mis trust

a buse

fear of exposure to

judg ments

mis in ter pre ta tions

did you peel

peel the learned

cos met ic   dis guises of so ci e ty

1995 Shirley A. Smith

Dedicated to me...............…..and you too…….....

Peel

peel away
all that hinders you
keeps you from dancing everyday
keeps you locked up tight
have you peeled
that which will not let you rest
the rewards are great
the hours are long
the work is tough
tears may you shed
hear yourself cry out
waiting for you
is the you
you never knew

peel

1995 Shirley A. Smith

www.ingramcontent.com/pod-product-compliance
Lightning Source LLC
Chambersburg PA
CBHW050947030426
42339CB00007B/318